KT-226-249

e.explore

Ancient Greece

Written by **Peter Chrisp**

e.explore

Ancient Greece

London, New York, Melbourne,
Munich, and Delhi

Project Editor Stephen Fall
Weblink Editors Niki Foreman, John Bennett, Clare Lister
Senior Editor Claire Nottage
Managing Editor Linda Esposito

Project Art Editor Steve Woosnam-Savage

Senior Art Editor Jim Green
Managing Art Editor Diane Thistlethwaite

DTP Co-ordinator Siu Chan

Consultant Dr Philip de Souza, University College Dublin

Jacket Copywriter Adam Powley
Jacket Editor Mariza O'Keeffe
Jacket Designer Neal Cobourne

Picture Research Sarah Hopper

Production Emma Hughes

Publishing Managers Andrew Macintyre,
Caroline Buckingham

Produced for DK by Toucan Books Ltd.
Managing Director Ellen Dupont

First published in Great Britain in 2006
by Dorling Kindersley Limited, 80 Strand, London WC2R 0RL

Penguin Group

Copyright © 2006 Dorling Kindersley Limited

Google™ is a trademark of Google Technology Inc.

2 4 6 8 10 9 7 5 3 1

All rights reserved. No part of this publication may be reproduced, stored in a
retrieval system, or transmitted in any form or by any means, electronic,
mechanical, photocopying, recording, or otherwise, without the prior written
permission of the copyright owner.

A CIP catalogue for this book is available from the British Library.

ISBN-13: 978-1-40531-345-2
ISBN-10: 1-4053-1345-5

Colour reproduction by Colourscan, Singapore
Printed in China by Toppan

Discover more at
www.dk.com

CONTENTS

How to use the e.explore website

e.explore Ancient Greece has its own website, created by DK and Google™. When you look up a subject in the book, the article gives you key facts and displays a keyword that links you to extra information online. Just follow these easy steps.

http://www.ancientgreece.dke-explore.com

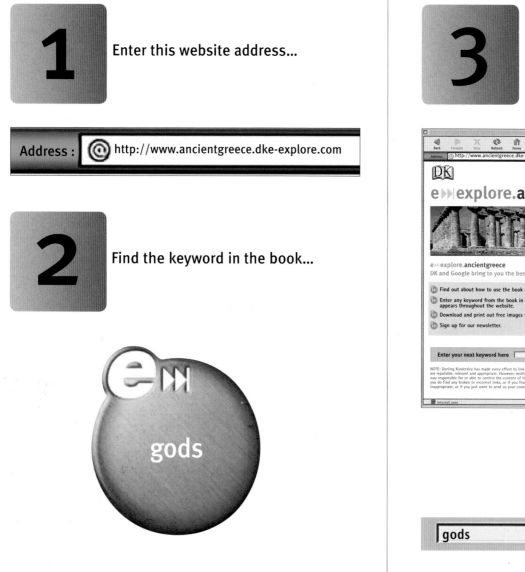

1 Enter this website address...

Address : @ http://www.ancientgreece.dke-explore.com

2 Find the keyword in the book...

gods

3 Enter the keyword...

gods

You can use only the keywords from the book to search on our website for the specially selected DK/Google links.

Be safe while you are online:

- Always get permission from an adult before connecting to the internet.

- Never give out personal information about yourself.

- Never arrange to meet someone you have talked to online.

- If a site asks you to log in with your name or email address, ask permission from an adult first.

- Do not reply to emails from strangers – tell an adult.

Parents: Dorling Kindersley actively and regularly reviews and updates the links. However, content may change. Dorling Kindersley is not responsible for any site but its own. We recommend that children are supervised while online, that they do not use Chat Rooms, and that filtering software is used to block unsuitable material.

4 Click on your chosen link...

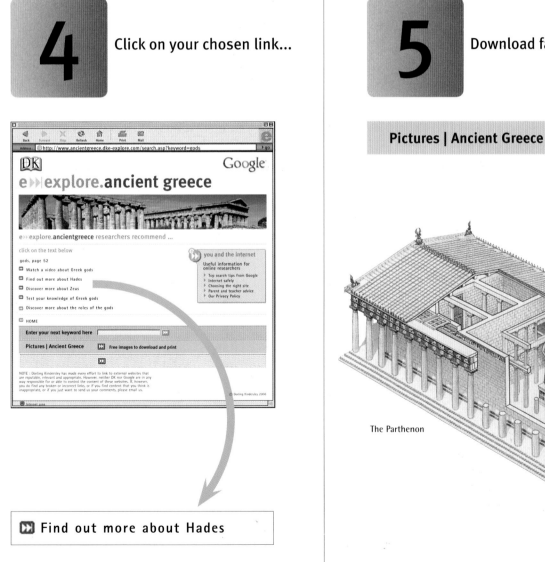

▶▶ Find out more about Hades

Links include animations, videos, sound buttons, virtual tours, interactive quizzes, databases, timelines, and realtime reports.

5 Download fantastic pictures...

Pictures | Ancient Greece ▶▶

The Parthenon

The pictures are free of charge, but can be used for personal, non-commercial use only.

Go back to the book for your next subject...

▲ THE GREEK WORLD
Greece has a mountainous mainland, with isolated plains, and hundreds of islands. The ancient Greeks also founded many settlements all over the Mediterranean.

THE SEA ▲
The Greeks lived close to the sea. This meant that they usually travelled by ship. Fish was more readily available than meat and formed a major part of their diet. This wall painting of a fisherman with a big catch comes from the island of Thera (now Santorini), and dates from around 1600 BC.

THE ANCIENT GREEKS

More than 2,500 years ago, the people of ancient Greece created one of the most advanced and influential civilizations of the world. Greek civilization reached a peak between 500 and 336 BC, a period called the Classical Age. The Greeks invented science, philosophy, theatre, and politics, and also introduced the alphabet to Europe. Greek stories are still told today, and their plays performed. They were also wonderful artists and builders whose temples, such as the Parthenon in Athens, are still considered to be some of the most beautiful buildings in the world.

▲ COMPETITIVE MEN
Greek men were among the most competitive people in history. They saw every activity, from sports to politics, as a competition, in which they tried to outdo each other and win glory. Cities also competed with each other and often went to war. Here an athlete, watched by his trainer, throws a discus.

CITY-STATES ▶
During the Classical Age, Greece was divided into hundreds of small *poleis*, or city-states. These divisions were partly due to the mountainous landscape. One of the most powerful *poleis* was Athens – now the capital of Greece. The modern city, still dominated by the ancient temple of Athena, has spread out, covering the plain where farmers once grew their crops.

STUDYING THE PAST

◄ STUDYING THE PAST
Thanks to their many writings, we know more about the Greeks than any other ancient people except the Romans. These works were carefully preserved and copied throughout the Middle Ages by Christian monks and Arab scholars. Letters and fragments of other texts have been discovered, preserved in the dry sand of Egypt. Further information about the Greeks comes from the archaeological excavations of Greek towns, tombs, temples, and shipwrecks. Here, archaeologists can be seen uncovering a mosaic of a god on the Greek island of Euboea.

Layers of sand are brushed away to reveal an ancient mosaic

GREEKS AND BARBARIANS ►
Although they were divided and competitive, the Greeks had a strong sense that they shared a culture which was better than all others. They worshipped the same gods and shared the same sacred places, such as Delphi, home of the god Apollo. Language also united them. Foreigners were called "barbarians" because their speech sounded like meaningless "bar bar" noises. Greeks thought that foreigners, such as the Persians on this vase, were less civilized than themselves.

King Darius of Persia depicted on a Greek vase

ancient Greeks

The Parthenon, temple of Athena (goddess of Athens)

Lycabettus, the highest point in Athens

GREEK HISTORY

BRONZE AGE (2900–1200 BC)
Greek history has been divided into five ages. The earliest is the Bronze Age, when bronze rather than iron was the main metal used. This was the period of the Minoan civilization of Crete, and the Mycenaean culture of mainland Greece. This Minoan wall painting shows a religious procession taking place.

DARK AGE (c.1200–800 BC)
After the Bronze Age civilizations were destroyed, Greece entered a "Dark Age", so-called because we know little about what was going on at this time. Unlike the Bronze Age Greeks, those of the Dark Age left no written records. A new Greek-speaking people arrived from the north, bringing iron-working with them.

ARCHAIC AGE (c.800–500 BC)
The Archaic ("old") Age was a time when Greek civilization slowly recovered. A new alphabet was introduced, and long-distance trade revived. The Greeks founded many overseas settlements throughout the Mediterranean. This was the period when the independent city-state, or *polis*, began to develop.

CLASSICAL AGE (c.500–336 BC)
During the Classical Age, Greek arts and architecture reached a peak. The two leading city-states, Athens and Sparta, were at the height of their powers. They joined together to fight off the Persian invasions, though they then went to war with each other. These ruins in Italy are a typical example of a classical temple.

HELLENISTIC AGE (336–150 BC)
During the Hellenistic ("Greek") age, the Greek states were united by King Alexander the Great of Macedon. He went on to conquer the Persian Empire, spreading the Greek way of life from Egypt to Afghanistan. His successors founded several large Hellenistic kingdoms, which were later conquered by the Romans.

THE MINOANS

On the large island of Crete, a wealthy, sophisticated civilization developed in the 3rd millennium BC, reaching a height between 2000 and 1500 BC. This civilization is called Minoan, after Minos, a legendary king who ruled at the city of Knossos in Crete. Although the Minoans were not Greeks, they had a big influence on early Greek life. The Minoans traded with the Greeks, who copied their art and their writing system. In about 1450 BC, Knossos was conquered by the Greeks, who later took over the whole island.

▲ DISCOVERY
Minoan civilization was discovered in the early 20th century when the English archaeologist Arthur Evans excavated a vast palace at Knossos. Soon after, similar buildings from the same period were found at Malia, Phaestos, and Zakro in Crete.

e ▶▶ Minoans

▲ THE FIRST WRITING
The need to organize society and keep accounts led to the invention of writing. Picture-based symbols were used at first, then these were simplified as lines, which were easier to write on clay tablets. This system, called Linear A, has not yet been deciphered, and we still do not know what language the Minoans spoke.

RECONSTRUCTION ▶
As well as excavating the Knossos palace, Evans also rebuilt parts of it to show how he thought the upper levels would have looked. He based this colonnade on the style of the columns seen in Minoan paintings.

Fresco (wall painting) of a bull

New wall built by Evans

Original wall of Knossos palace, uncovered by Evans

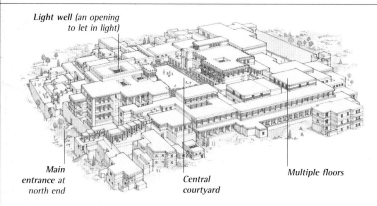

THE PALACE OF KNOSSOS

Light well (an opening to let in light)

Main entrance at north end

Central courtyard

Multiple floors

As well as being a grand palace, Knossos was also a religious centre and operated as a seat of government that ruled over large areas of Crete. The vast, sprawling palace was filled with workshops used by metalworkers and other craftsmen, and also served as a warehouse, with storage areas for grain, olive oil, and wine. It even had its own advanced plumbing and drainage system, used to take away waste materials from the site. Archaeological investigation has revealed that, in total, the entire complex covered an area of about 13,000 sq m (140,000 sq ft).

Seated cat

Tight bodice and belt

Flounces
(overlapping strips of cloth)

◄ SNAKE HANDLER

At Knossos, Evans found a pottery figurine of a woman handling two snakes, which was made around 1600 BC. Snakes were sacred to the Greeks as guardian figures and were associated with powers beneath the earth. The animals connected with this woman suggest that this is no ordinary person, but a goddess. The figurine helps us to learn about the clothes worn by wealthy Minoan women.

▲ THE BULL LEAPERS

This wall painting from Knossos shows a sport or religious ritual in which young Minoans leap over the back of a bull. Bulls seem to have been sacred to the Minoans and often appear in their art. Bull leaping may be connected to the origin of later Greek legends of the Minotaur – a half-man, half-bull monster that was said to have lived at Knossos.

SEAFARERS ►

The Minoans were great traders who sailed all around the eastern Mediterranean. They exported vases and imported raw materials, such as copper, tin, and ivory, needed for the craft workshops of the palaces. This wall painting, from Akrotiri on the island of Thera (Santorini), shows what a Minoan fleet would have looked like. The people of Akrotiri may either have been Cretan settlers, or possibly locals influenced by the ways of the Minoans.

Perching birds indicate this was a goddess

FIGURINE FOUND AT KARPHI

▲ HOLY MOUNTAIN

On the peak of Mount Juktas, overlooking Knossos, the Minoans set up an outdoor religious sanctuary. Here they worshipped their gods and left behind offerings, such as pottery figurines. Mountaintops were also sacred to later Greeks, who believed these were the home of their gods.

THE END OF THE MINOANS ►

Minoan civilization came to an end between 1250–1200 BC, when all the palaces were abandoned. The cause was probably a foreign invasion, for the whole eastern Mediterranean was in turmoil at this time. The Minoans retreated to remote mountain areas, such as Karphi, where they continued to leave offerings to their gods until about 1050 BC.

THE MYCENAEANS

The people who lived in mainland Greece during the Bronze Age are known as Mycenaeans, after Mycenae, their most important centre. The lifestyle and culture of the Minoans greatly influenced them. The Mycenaeans adapted Minoan script to write Greek and copied Minoan fashions, pottery, jewellery, and wall paintings. The Mycenaeans were a much more warlike people than the Minoans, however, and by the 14th century BC they had become the leading power in the eastern Mediterranean.

Irregularly shaped blocks lock together

FORTIFICATIONS ▲
Although Mycenaean palaces are much smaller than Minoan ones, far more work went into fortifying them. Massive walls up to 7 m (23 ft) thick, suggest that war was common. The stones in these fortifications, at Tiryns, fit together like jigsaw pieces to make the walls even stronger. Later Greeks called the walls "Cyclopean" because they imagined that they were built by giants called *cyclopes*.

Heads of lions (now missing) stared straight out at visitors

▲ PALACES
The Mycenaeans lived in small kingdoms centred on palaces, such as those at Pylos and Tiryns (in southern Greece), and Mycenae and Thebes. Each palace had a *megaron*, or hall, with a central, round hearth surrounded by four great columns. The *megaron* was where the *wanax*, or king, held court. This is an artist's impression of the richly decorated *megaron* at Pylos.

Beaten gold was used for the mask

ROYAL GOLD ▶
The Mycenaean kings were extremely rich and were buried with vast amounts of gold. The "mask of Agamemnon" was named after the legendary king of Mycenae. It was discovered in 1876 by a German archaeologist, Heinrich Schliemann, who thought that it proved Agamemnon really had existed. Researchers now believe the mask dates from before Agamemnon might have lived, but it has retained the king's name.

Lintel stone is 4.5 m (nearly 15 ft) long and weighs about 18 tonnes (tons)

◄ ROYAL TOMBS

Mycenaean kings displayed their power and wealth by building dome-shaped *tholos* tombs. This one at Mycenae is the largest, with stones carefully shaped to create inwardly curving walls. The doorway is 5.5 m (18 ft) high, and it is estimated that the massive lintel stone above it weighs 120 tonnes (tons). The tomb was built between 1330 and 1250 BC, when Mycenae was at the height of its power.

▲ HUNTING

Alongside warfare, hunting was a favourite subject in Mycenaean art. Nobles hunted boar and lions, which were then still living wild in Greece. They did this with spears and shields, the same equipment they used in battle, so hunting also offered useful training for warfare. This bronze dagger showing a lion hunt was decorated with gold and silver. It is a fine example of the skill of Mycenaean artists.

Mycenaean hunters approaching a lion

▼ THE LION GATE

The Lion Gate was the entrance to the palace at Mycenae. This gate holds the oldest piece of monumental sculpture in Europe. Its triangular limestone slab is carved with two lions on either side of a pillar – an image that also appears on seal stones. This may have been the royal family's coat-of-arms. Another interpretation is that the lions were sacred to the chief Mycenaean god.

Mycenaeans

Boars' tusks in rows

Shaped block fits around sculpture

◄ HELMET AND ARMOUR

Wild boar were hunted not just for their meat but also for their tusks. These were sewn onto leather linings to make helmets. Tusks offered better protection than bronze – a relatively soft metal. A tusk helmet was also worn as a sign of high status, since it took 30 to 40 animals to make just one. This helmet, along with the body armour made from overlapping bronze plates, was found in a warrior's tomb at Dendra (near Argos). This is the world's oldest known suit of armour.

LINEAR B

Thousands of clay tablets with writing on have been found in Mycenaean palaces. Mycenaean writing is called Linear B (a later form than Linear A—the undeciphered Minoan script). In 1951-3, English cryptographer Michael Ventris deciphered Linear B. It was used to write an early form of Greek.

Linear B writing used in a financial record

HOMER AND THE TROJAN WAR

Mycenaean civilization collapsed around 1200 BC, when the palaces were destroyed. Knowledge of writing was lost until a new alphabet was created in the 8th century BC. Mycenaean history was preserved through Greek stories, told and passed on by each generation. The most famous tells of a ten-year war fought by the Greeks against Troy – a city thought to be in what is now Turkey. This formed the basis for two long poems, Homer's *Iliad* and *Odyssey* – the closest things to sacred texts that the Greeks possessed.

BRONZE FIGURINE WITH A LYRE

▲ RHAPSODES
Homer's poems were memorized by professional reciters called *rhapsodes*. They performed the poems at festivals where they competed for prizes. Early *rhapsodes* accompanied themselves on a lyre. Filled with emotion as they recited, they hoped to inspire the same emotions in their audience.

▲ HOMER
Homer is thought to have lived in Ionia (now on the coast of Turkey) at some time during the 8th century BC. He was working at the end of a long tradition of Greek oral poets – men who recited their works to an audience from memory. We do not know whether Homer could write, but he was probably the person who composed and shaped the stories into dramatic poems.

Trojan War

Quiver for arrows or a gorytos *(combined arrow and bow case)*

KYLIX (WINE CUP) MADE IN ATHENS IN ABOUT 500 BC

WAS THERE REALLY A TROJAN WAR?

In the 19th century AD, Heinrich Schliemann set out to prove that the Trojan War really did take place. He searched for the site of Troy, the approximate location of which had been known since ancient times. In Hisarlik in Turkey, Schliemann uncovered a Bronze Age citadel that had been destroyed and rebuilt many times. This may well have been the city of Troy, but whether or not it was ever attacked by a Greek army led by Agamemnon, the legendary king of Mycenae, is something that historians will probably never know.

◄ ANGRY ACHILLES
Homer's *Iliad* recounts a single episode lasting a few weeks out of the ten-year war. The subject is the anger of Achilles, the greatest of the Greek heroes. Achilles sulks in his tent after a quarrel with Agamemnon, his commander-in-chief. When his best friend, Patroclus, is killed by the Trojan hero Hector, Achilles' anger turns against the Trojans. He returns to the fight and kills Hector in single combat. This painting shows him tenderly bandaging a wound on Patroclus' arm after an earlier fight.

ODYSSEUS' HELMET ▶

Homer's works were set in the past and preserve many details of the Bronze Age, even though he lived five centuries later. For example, the warriors in Homer's writings fight with bronze weapons rather than the iron of his day. Odysseus is even described as wearing a helmet covered in "rows of white tusks from a shining-toothed boar", although such armour was used hundreds of years previously. In their original form, the stories may date back to the Mycenaean period, and poets such as Homer might have performed them in Mycenaean palaces. This helmet, found in a Mycenaean warrior's grave, matches Homer's description of it exactly.

Wild boar tusks

HELMET FROM THE 13TH CENTURY BC

▼ THE TROJAN HORSE

Homer's story is still being told today. This scene from the 2004 Hollywood film *Troy* shows the city being captured. The Greeks pretend to sail home and leave behind a wooden horse as a supposed peace offering. The Trojans bring the horse into their city, unaware that a group of Greek warriors is hiding inside. At night the warriors creep out to open the gates of Troy and let in the Greek army.

THE WANDERINGS OF ODYSSEUS

▲ SIRENS

The *Odyssey* is the story of the adventures of the hero Odysseus on his way home after the war. He survives perils such as the sirens – creatures whose singing can lure sailors to their doom. Odysseus makes his men block their ears, but he has himself tied to the mast so he can hear the beautiful song without dying.

▲ CYCLOPS

Odysseus and his men are imprisoned in a cave by the cyclops Polyphemus, a one-eyed giant. Odysseus gets Polyphemus drunk and blinds him with a hot wooden stake. As Odysseus recalls, "We twirled it in his eye, and the blood boiled around the hot point . . . and the fire made the roots of his eye crackle."

▲ HOME AT LAST

This relief shows one of the most moving scenes in the *Odyssey* – Odysseus' homecoming to Ithaca after 20 years away. Disguised as a beggar, he is reunited with his wife Penelope, who does not yet realize he is her husband, and who "weeps for the man, who was there by her side".

MYTHS AND HEROES

There are hundreds of ancient Greek myths. Deriving from the word *mythos* ("word", "speech", or "message"), myths were traditional stories told by the Greeks. These stories explained relationships between men and women, how cities were created, and why religious rituals were performed. Myths also tell the stories of the gods. Every Greek knew the stories, which they first heard as children from their mothers and nurses. Poets acted out the myths at festivals, and women told them to each other as they wove.

▲ JASON AND THE GOLDEN FLEECE
Myths often tell of a hero's quest and the ordeals he goes through before claiming his rightful inheritance. Jason was the son of King Aeson of Iolcus (in Thessaly), who was driven out of his kingdom by his half-brother, Pelias. When Jason came to claim his inheritance, Pelias tried to get rid of him by sending him on a quest to find a golden fleece (sheepskin) guarded by a dragon. Jason won the help of a sorceress, Medea, who used magic to send the dragon to sleep. In this painting, Jason stands over the sleeping dragon and reaches towards the fleece.

The Minotaur is captured and killed by Theseus

◄ THESEUS AND THE MINOTAUR
Theseus was the son of King Aegeus of Athens. According to the myth, each year the Athenians sent 14 young men and women to King Minos of Crete. Minos forced them into a labyrinth, or maze, to be eaten by the Minotaur – a monster which was half-man and half-bull. Theseus offered to join the victims so he could kill the monster. Ariadne, the daughter of Minos, fell in love with Theseus and gave him a sword and a ball of string. After tying one end of the string to the entrance of the labyrinth, Theseus went inside and killed the Minotaur, then successfully found his way out again by following the string back to the entrance.

myths and heroes

Offerings left at a shrine

ZEUS'S TEMPLE
AT NEMEA

▲ THE POWERFUL DEAD

Greeks thought their local heroes, such as Theseus, had the power to help or harm the living. There was a saying that you should not eat food which fell on the floor because "it belongs to the heroes". The heroes had shrines, often on the site of their supposed tombs, where people left offerings.

◄ BABY HERO

At Nemea in the Peloponnese, there was a shrine to a baby hero called Opheltes. Apollo's priestess said it was dangerous for Opheltes to touch the ground before he could walk. His nurse disobeyed the priestess and placed Opheltes on the ground, and the baby was killed by a snake. The Nemean games were held for his funeral, so he is known as the founder of these games.

◄ HERACLES

The greatest hero of all was Heracles. He was the son of a human mother, Alcmene, and Zeus, the king of the gods. After his death he was believed to be a god. Unlike other heroes, who were only worshipped locally, Heracles was worshipped throughout Greece. He was famous for his superhuman strength, which he used to perform 12 labours (difficult tasks), set for him by King Eurystheus of Mycenae and Tiryns. Eurystheus sent him on difficult quests in areas around the Peloponnese hoping that Heracles would get killed. Eurystheus was afraid that Heracles, who was his cousin, wanted to replace him as king.

Lion's head

SOME OF HERACLES' LABOURS

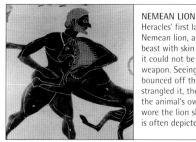

NEMEAN LION
Heracles' first labour was to kill the Nemean lion, a huge, ferocious beast with skin so tough that it could not be pierced by any weapon. Seeing that his arrows bounced off the lion, Heracles strangled it, then skinned it using the animal's own claws. He later wore the lion skin as armour (and is often depicted this way in art).

THE HYDRA
Next, Heracles had to kill the Hydra of Lerna a poisonous, snake-like creature with many heads. When he cut off the heads, new ones kept growing in their place. Heracles eventually killed the Hydra by shooting it with arrows he had dipped in its blood, which was even more poisonous than the creature's venom.

THE ERYMANTHIAN BOAR
After Heracles had killed the Hydra, King Eurystheus ordered him to catch a gigantic wild boar that lived on Mount Erymanthus, where it often attacked and killed the local people. After trapping the marauding animal in a net, Heracles brought it back to the king, who was so frightened that he hid inside a large pot.

CERYNITIAN STAG
Heracles' fourth labour was to catch the Cerynitian stag – a beautiful male deer with golden horns, which was sacred to the goddess Artemis. The stag was not dangerous, just extremely hard to catch. It took Heracles a year to track the animal down. After bringing the stag back to show Eurystheus, he set it free.

THE STYMPHALIAN BIRDS
The next monsters killed by Heracles were man-eating birds living at Lake Stymphalus. The birds had bronze feathers which they could fire like arrows. Heracles shook a bronze rattle, given to him by the god Hephaestus, which made the birds fly up into the air. He then shot them with his bow and arrows.

THE DARK AGE

The Mycenaean period ended in about 1200 BC, when the palaces were destroyed – possibly due to rebellions, war between kingdoms, or a foreign invasion. A period now known as the Dark Age followed. Far less is known about life in Greece at this time because the knowledge of writing was lost. Sea trading also declined. The population dropped greatly compared to that in Mycenaean times. Most people needed to grow and farm their own food to survive – the age of palaces and wealthy merchants was over. At this point, a new Greek-speaking people called the Dorians arrived from the north-west of the country.

▲ WARFARE
Like the Mycenaeans, the Greeks of the Dark Age were ruled by an aristocratic class of warriors, men who were rich enough to afford horses and good quality weapons. This vase shows a warrior riding a chariot, pulled by a pair of horses. The cartoon-like style of the figures is much simpler than that found in Mycenaean art.

◄ SONS OF HERACLES
The Dorians settled in the Peloponnese, in the south of the Greek mainland. They later invented their own myth to explain their arrival, and to justify their rule there. According to the myth, their kings were descended from Heracles, whose sons had been exiled by Eurystheus. The Dorians thought their invasion marked the return of the *Heraclidae* (the descendants of Heracles), who had come back to claim their land.

Dark Age

Ironworker (or smith)   Metal bar   Boy pumping bellows

Clay furnace

◄ IRON WORKING
The Dorians brought with them the knowledge of working iron. They used the metal to make swords, tools, and cloak pins. Iron is a harder metal than bronze, and so better for making weapons. It was more readily available, but required a much higher temperature to work than bronze. Iron was heated with charcoal in a furnace built of brick and lined with clay, then hammered at a forge to shape it and remove impurities. The iron object was then plunged into cold water to harden it. This vase painting shows an ironworker at his furnace.

Lions' mouths, open as if roaring

IONIANS ▶

the Dorians arrived, many original
tants of the Greek mainland moved
ss the sea to live on the islands and
on the coast of Asia Minor (modern
key). The largest group were named
Ionians, after Ion – a mythical hero
they believed was their ancestor. The
s assembled every year on the island
elos, birthplace of the god Apollo, to
rate his festival. Dorian Greeks were
llowed to attend. These marble lions
ere a gift to Apollo from the Ionians
Naxos. They guard the sacred lake on
Delos where Apollo was born. These
are modern copies – the original
sculptures are kept in the
museum on Delos.

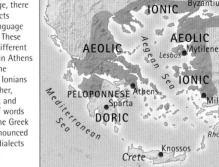

GREEK DIALECTS

By the end of the Dark Age, there
were three different dialects
(versions) of the Greek language
– Doric, Ionic, and Aeolic. These
developed differently in different
areas – Ionic was spoken in Athens
while Doric was used in the
Peloponnese. Dorians and Ionians
could understand each other,
but had different accents, and
slightly different forms of words
– in Doric, for example, the Greek
word for mother was pronounced
"mater", while the other dialects
pronounced it as "meter".

*Marble weathered
by wind and rain*

ABSTRACT PATTERNS

DECORATED POTS
In the Dark Age, the Greeks continued
the Mycenaean practice of burying
their dead with pottery goods. These
were often decorated with neat patterns
rather than with pictures. This pot is
painted with rows of horizontal
lines and a series of waves.

WINE JUG
The Greeks invented many types of
painted pottery, each for a special
purpose. A few were made for display,
but most had a practical use. This is an
oinochoe, which has a handle and spout
for pouring wine. It was created on a
potter's wheel in about 730 BC.

▲ A NEW SCRIPT
From 800 BC, Greek civilization was revived, as the Greeks began to trade with
the Middle East again. It was there that they came across a new writing system,
developed by the Phoenicians. The Phoenician alphabet only had signs for
consonants. The Greeks adapted this to write their own language, by adding extra
signs for vowels. It had only 24 letters so was easier to learn than the Linear B
alphabet, which had 87 signs. Early Greek writing appears on this vase.

Acropolis of Corinth
reaches high above
the temple

Ruined temple
of Apollo

RISE OF THE POLIS

The Greek *polis*, or city-state, was a system of government
developed at the end of the Dark Age. By this time, the Greeks
lived in hundreds of *poleis*. Each *polis* included the city and
the countryside around it and operated as a separate state with
its own calendar, laws, public assemblies, and coins. *Poleis*
came in many sizes. The tiniest was the island of Delos, at
five sq km (two sq miles) of land. Athens ruled 2,600 sq km
(1,000 sq miles) and was one of the biggest.

▲ ACROPOLIS
A *polis* usually had a high fortified area called an
acropolis ("high city"). This was where the most
important temples were often built. It was also a
place to take refuge if the *polis* was ever attacked.
The acropolis with the best defences was the one at
Corinth, towering 565 m (1,854 ft) above the city.

LAWGIVERS ▶
The citizens of *poleis* often appointed lawgivers to draw up public law codes.
Solon (c.640-560 BC), the lawgiver of Athens, drew up laws limiting the power of
the aristocracy, and he abolished the harsh punishments of an earlier lawgiver,
Draco. Asked whether he had written the best laws for the Athenians, Solon
replied, "The best they would accept". In this painting he can be seen
defending his laws against objections from rich fellow citizens.

South stoa, where
friends met and
business was done

Hellaia, Athens'
main law court

Bouleuterion, where the
city council met

Temple of Hephaestus,
god of metalworkers

◀ AGORA
The city centre was the *agora*, or marketplace,
where people met to do business every day.
This was also the political and legal heart of
the *polis*. It was surrounded by civic buildings,
including lawcourts and meeting places for the
boule ("city council"). Here, long colonnaded
buildings called *stoas* provided shade from
the summer sun and shelter on wet or windy
days. This artist's impression shows the *agora* of
Athens. At the top left is a hill called the *Pnyx*,
where public assemblies of citizens gathered.

Market stalls with
awnings for shade

Ivy wreath

◄ TYRANTS
In certain *poleis*, individuals were able to seize power, ruling as tyrants. This did not originally mean a cruel ruler, and many tyrants were thought of as good. Peisistratos of Athens (who reigned 546–527 BC) created new religious festivals, built fine temples, and oversaw the first standard version of Homer's writings (which had previously existed in various versions). Dionysius I of Syracuse (who reigned 406–367 BC), was a brilliant general as well as being a patron of the arts.

DIONYSIUS I

city state

◄ KINGS AND OFFICIALS
Once ruled by a king, the *polis* was now governed instead by elected officials, and thought to belong to a local god. In Athens, for example, the god was Athena. Sparta was the exception. The city kept its kings – albeit with limited powers. The Spartan kings had prestige because they were supposed to have descended from Heracles.

STATUE OF ATHENA
(FROM HER TEMPLE
IN ATHENS)

Dagger

ARISTOGEITON   HARMODIUS

Broken sword

TYRANNICIDES ►
Tyrants were sometimes able to hand on power to their sons, but tyranny rarely lasted more than two generations. The sons of Peisistratos – Hippias and Hipparchus – were unpopular rulers. In 514 BC, the Athenians Aristogeiton and Harmodius tried to murder them, but were themselves killed after assassinating Hipparchus. When Hippias was finally driven out, in 510 BC, the *tyrannicides* (tyrant killers) were celebrated as heroes.

COINS

ATHENA'S OWL
Each city minted its own coins, and these were decorated with an emblem linked with the city. Athens, for example, had a coin showing Athena on one side, and an owl on the other. Because of their big, watchful eyes, owls were thought to be wise, and therefore were sacred to Athena, the goddess of wisdom.

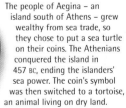

AEGINA'S TURTLE
The people of Aegina – an island south of Athens – grew wealthy from sea trade, so they chose to put a sea turtle on their coins. The Athenians conquered the island in 457 BC, ending the islanders' sea power. The coin's symbol was then switched to a tortoise, an animal living on dry land.

WINGED HORSE OF CORINTH
The emblem on a coin sometimes showed a myth connected with the *polis*. Corinth's coins showed Pegasus, the winged horse that was caught and tamed by the hero Bellerophon on top of Corinth's acropolis. Greek coins were copied and used by other Mediterranean peoples. This coin showing Pegasus is from Carthage in north Africa.

EUROPE
GAUL
Alps
Rhone
Pyrenees
Massalia
IBERIA Emporion
Corsica
ITALY
Rome
Tarentum
Hemeroscopium
Mainaca
Balearic
Islands
Sardinia
Tyrrhenian
Sea
Sicily Syracuse
Chaeronea Thebes
Megara Athens
Sparta Corinth
Mediterranean Sea
Cyrene
AFRICA
Donube
Adriatic Sea
GREECE
Olbia
Istros
Black Sea
Byzantium
Mytilene ASIA MINOR
Miletus
Euphrates
Rhodes
Crete Cyprus
Naucratis
Nile
Red
Sea

◄ SETTLEMENTS
Between 750 and 400 BC, dozens of
Greek *poleis* were founded all around
the Mediterranean and the Black Sea.
These included far-flung settlements
such as Massalia (Marseilles) on the coast
of Gaul (France), Cyrene in North Africa,
Naucratis in Egypt, Istrus and Olbia on
the Black Sea, and Emporion (Ampurias)
in Spain. The largest
number of settlements
was in southern Italy
and Sicily, which the
Romans came to
call Magna Graecia
(Great Greece).

overseas

THE GREEKS OVERSEAS

A continual problem facing the Greeks was shortage of
good farmland. When the population grew too big for
the local land to support, the citizens were forced to
make new settlements overseas. Settlements were
also established as a result of political struggles
within *poleis* that often created exiles who needed
to find a new home. Each settlement became
an independent *polis*. Thus the founders
of Syracuse in Italy, who originally
came from Corinth, stopped being
Corinthian citizens and became
citizens of the new *polis*.

*Columns of rough, orange-
coloured, local limestone*

◄ GOD OF CITY FOUNDING
Apollo was the god of founding new cities.
Having decided to found a new settlement,
a *polis* would send messengers to the god's
temple at Delphi to ask for his approval, which
was given by his priestess. When the first Greeks
arrived in Sicily and founded the *polis* of Naxos,
one of the first things they did was to build an altar
to Apollo Archegetes (the founder), where they
could offer sacrifices to him.

FOUNDER ▲
The man in charge of organizing a new settlement was called an
oikist. In Athens, these were state officials who then returned home
again after finishing the task. Alternatively, a group of settlers
would invite a highly regarded Greek to become their *oikist*. After
death, city-founders were treated as godlike heroes, celebrated
on coins and in statues, and offered sacrifices. Historians such as
Thucydides recorded their names. Akragas (or Agrigento) in Sicily
(*above*), founded around 582 BC, had two *oikists*, Aristonous and
Pystilus. Both came from Gela in Sicily. Gela was itself founded 108
years earlier, by Antiphemus from Rhodes and Entimus from Crete.

PLANNING A SETTLEMENT ►
The decision to found a new *polis* involved enormous expense. The settlers had to be provided with ships, food, and weapons, in case they had to fight the local inhabitants. Settlers were carefully chosen and included skilled builders, land surveyors, priests, and craftworkers. They sailed until they found a suitable place. A sheltered harbour, a defensible acropolis, a supply of fresh water, and good farmland where they could grow olive trees (*right*) and other crops were all desirable.

◄ AFRICAN GREEKS
The settlement of Cyrene in North Africa grew rich exporting a local herb called *silphium*, valued as an all-purpose medicine throughout the Greek world. *Silphium* was in great demand and by the 1st century AD, the Greeks of Cyrene had harvested so much that the plant died out. Coins such as this one show us what *silphium* looked like.

◄ OLIVES AND VINES
This vase shows men harvesting olives. Along with grapes, this was the Greeks' most important crop, and they took both with them everywhere. They introduced vines and olives to southern France, where they traded wine with the local Gauls for tin. The first wine in France was Greek and made in Massalia (Marseilles).

TEMPLE OF HERA IN AGRIGENTO, SICILY

ROMANS ►
In Italy, the Hellenes, as Greeks called themselves, first met the Romans, who asked the newcomers where they were from. Instead of answering "We are Hellenes", they replied "We come from Graia", the *polis* they had just left. Due to a misunderstanding, the Romans began to call all Hellenes "Graeci" (Greeks). The Greek influence on the Romans can be seen on this mirror lid showing the Roman goddess Venus, identified with the Greek Aphrodite.

◄ SOFT SYBARITES
"Sybarite" is a name given to someone devoted to pleasure. The settlement of Sybaris in Italy was famous for the wealth and luxurious standard of living of its people. Sybarites spent their lives enjoying themselves with drinking parties, like the one shown on this cup. In 572 BC, Smindyrides, a Sybarite, travelled to Greece to marry a tyrant's daughter. Worried that the food would not be up to his usual standards, he brought with him a thousand attendants, including fishermen, fowlers (wild-bird hunters), and cooks.

ATHENS

The largest and richest *polis* on the Greek mainland was Athens, which was Greece's leading artistic and intellectual centre. Many of the most famous Greek writers and sculptors were Athenians, and the city itself was filled with beautiful public buildings, including the world's first theatre. Yet the most striking thing about the Athenians was the way they governed themselves. Shortly after the overthrow of the last tyrant in 510 BC, the Athenians invented a new system they called "democracy" ("people power"). Every citizen, whether rich or poor, now had a say in how Athens was run.

ACROPOLIS ▲

The most sacred buildings in Athens were those on the rock of the Acropolis. These included the temple to Athena, which held an ancient olive-wood statue of the goddess, believed to have fallen from the sky. The rock itself was regarded as a holy place. In mythology, it was where the gods Poseidon and Athena competed for possession of the city. Athena won by planting an olive tree – the first in the world.

WOMAN WINDING WOOL

▲ SPEAKER'S PLATFORM

The *bema*, or speaker's platform on the Pnyx hill, was where the Athenian citizens' assembly regularly gathered to make decisions about the running of the *polis*. Every citizen over the age of 18 had the right to make a speech here and to vote. Most other Greek *poleis* were oligarchies (which means "rule by the few"), where only the wealthiest citizens had power. Rich Greeks hated Athenian democracy. A writer known only as the Old Oligarch complained that the Athenians preferred "the interests of the mob to those of respectable people".

Bema *(speaker's platform) carved out of the bedrock*

CITIZENS ▶

Only men whose parents were both Athenian citizens had full political rights. Citizens did not include slaves or *metics* (Greeks from other cities who came to live in Athens). Athenian women also had reduced rights. Although they were regarded as citizens they could not speak at the public assemblies or vote.

Oarsmen

◄ SEA POWER

Athens was a great naval power, owning one of the largest war fleets in Greece. In the early 5th century BC, the city had 200 warships, called *triremes*, each powered by 170 oarsmen. *Trireme* means "fitted with three", referring to the three banks of seating where the oarsmen sat.

TEMPLE BUILT
C.450–440 BC

Trireme

Olive leaf

SILVER ►

Much of the city's wealth came from the state-owned silver mines at Laureion, which were worked by slaves. This silver was used to make the city's coins, bearing Athena's sacred owl and a sprig of her sacred olive tree. Thanks to the silver, the Athenians were able to build their fleet, and pay the wages of 34,000 oarsmen. There were not enough Athenians to man the ships, so Greeks from many islands came to Piraeus (the port of Athens) to seek work in the Athenian navy.

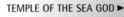

Athens

TEMPLE OF THE SEA GOD ►

When the Athenian fleet sailed to war, the ships passed Poseidon's temple (*right*), which overlooked the sea at Cape Sounion. Looking up at its white columns, the commanders would offer a prayer to Poseidon, asking for a safe voyage. The Athenian writer Thucydides described a great fleet setting off in 415 BC: "The officers and men made their libations from cups of gold and silver . . . When the hymn had been sung and the libations finished, they put out to sea, first sailing in a column, and then racing each other."

ARTISTIC CENTRE

POTTERY

As a famous artistic centre, Athens produced beautiful pottery, which was exported throughout the Greek world. This is an Attic (Athenian) *krater*, a large vase used for mixing wine and water. It is decorated with a painting of gods in procession on Mount Olympus. This is called "red figure ware", a style invented in Athens.

Columns are 6 m (20 ft) high

SCULPTURE

Sculptures were either carved from marble or cast with molten bronze that was poured into a mould. Bronzes, such as this horse, were as common in Athens as statues carved from marble. Today, however, they are very rare because often the metal was melted down to be reused.

TERRACOTTA FIGURES

Terracotta (fired red clay) was used to make small models showing scenes from daily life. These were used as decorations for the home. This terracotta figure shows a young woman playing with the knucklebones of a sheep or pig. They were thrown like dice, or tossed in the air and caught on the back of the hand.

DEMOCRACY

Every male citizen of Athens played a part in how the city was governed. All public offices were filled by ordinary citizens, usually chosen by lot. This was thought to be more democratic than elections, which could favour those who were well known. Every important decision was made by the assembly (*ekklesia*), where all the citizens could speak and vote. Ordinary citizens also served as jurors in trials and soldiers in wartime. It was both an honour and a duty to serve the *polis* in these ways.

▲ THE ASSEMBLY
Every nine days or so, there was a huge public assembly held in the open air on the Pnyx hill. Every citizen had the right to speak and vote on important issues, such as whether to go to war or to build a new temple. If a major decision needed to be made, at least 6,000 citizens were required to be present.

democracy

STRATEGOI ▶
Ten *strategoi* (generals) were elected to command the army. Choosing experienced commanders was very important. It was possible to be re-elected year after year, and some *strategoi* became very politically powerful. The most famous was Pericles, who dominated Athens for years. His power came from an ability to win over the assembly with speeches.

Tholos, *thought to be a dining room for the* boule

Bouleuterion *where the* boule *held its meetings*

▲ THE COUNCIL
A *boule*, or council, of 500 men drew up proposals to be debated by the assembly. The *boule* also received ambassadors and negotiated with foreign states. Members were chosen each year by drawing lots. They could serve only twice, and not in consecutive years. In order that the poorest citizens could also serve, payment was introduced in the 5th century BC. The council met in a building called the *bouleuterion*, which contained the state archives – records of treaties, court cases, laws passed by the assembly, and oracles given to Athens.

Laws were engraved in stone at Delphi

Cracks in restored clay water clock

LAWS ▲
There were no professional judges or lawyers in Athens. Every citizen had the right to bring another citizen to trial, and also to serve on a jury. To prevent bribery, juries were large, with between 101 and 1,001 men, depending on the seriousness of the case. Every citizen was expected to have a good understanding of the laws, which were displayed on stone tablets in the *agora*.

Slots for bronze jurors' tickets

Hole indicates token was used to vote for innocence

▲ TRIALS
A complicated method was used to select jurors in order to prevent the accused identifying them in advance and bribing them. They were chosen at the last moment, using a machine called a *kleroterion*. White and black pebbles were dropped into a tube. These were then matched against the names of jurors on bronze tickets placed in the slots.

▲ WATER CLOCK
Trials took the form of opposing speeches made by the accuser and the accused. To make sure that each side had the same amount of time in which to speak, the speeches were carefully timed with a water clock, which used two bowls. Each speech could only last as long as the water took to flow from the upper bowl into the lower one.

▲ VERDICTS
In the 5th century BC, jurors gave their verdicts using white and black pebbles. In the 4th century BC, these were replaced by bronze tokens – a token with a solid centre meant "guilty", whilst a hollow centre stood for "innocent". Jurors marched past two urns, dropping the token to be counted into one and the token to be discarded into another.

◄ OSTRACISM
Ostracism, a word we still use today, meant the exiling of unpopular politicians for a period of ten years. The citizens wrote the name of the man they wished to exile on a piece of pottery called an *ostrakon*. A minimum of 6,000 men were needed for an ostracism to be valid, and if enough *ostraka* were collected against a man, he had to leave the city within ten days. This *ostrakon* bears the name of Aristeides – a leading Athenian general ostracized in 483 BC.

Socrates drinking hemlock

Inscription names Aristeides, son of Lysimachus, for exile

Weeping friends watch helplessly

PUNISHMENTS ►
There were fixed punishments for some offences while others had to be decided by the jury, with another vote. Punishments included exile, fines, and even death. In 399 BC, the philosopher Socrates was sentenced to death for being a bad influence on the young men of Athens. Although he had the chance to escape, he refused to flee because of his respect for the laws of Athens. Instead, he drank hemlock (a type of poison) and waited calmly for his death.

SPARTA

The great rival of Athens was Sparta, which was unlike any other *polis*. The Spartans were full-time soldiers, members of the only professional army in Greece. Sparta had two kings, from two royal families, who ruled alongside a council of 28 elders. The powers of the kings were limited by five *ephors* ("overseers"), who could arrest and depose them. *Ephors*, who were elected each year, oversaw the day-to-day running of the state. Although assemblies were held, the citizens could not speak. Instead, they accepted or rejected decisions made by the *ephors*, kings, and council, by shouting.

▲ KINGS
Spartan kings were generals in wartime – marching in front of the army, and performing sacrifices before battle. At home, they performed religious duties. Dual kingship also limited their power. It was difficult for one king to act against the wishes of the other.

TRAINING FOR WAR ▶
Spartan men spent their days in training for war – exercising, practising with weapons, and marching in tight ranks to the music of a pipe. The Greek writer Plutarch wrote that the Spartans were the only men in the world for whom fighting wars was a welcome rest from training for war! This is a modern statue of a famous Spartan king, Leonidas, who died in battle with all his men, while defending Greece against Persian invaders.

Usually, Spartans expected to win their battles. If they were outnumbered, as Leonidas was, they were expected to die fighting rather than surrender.

▲ RUINS OF SPARTA
Sparta was little more than a collection of five villages in the valley of the Eurotas river. Unlike Athens, with its beautiful temples, Sparta today has few archaeological remains. The Athenian historian, Thucydides, predicted that this would be the case. He wrote, "Suppose . . . that the city of Sparta became deserted and only the temples and foundations of buildings remained, I think that future generations would, as time passed, find it very difficult to believe that the place had really been as powerful as it was represented to be."

*Leonidas' shield,
raised to protect
his body*

Sparta

Zeus
Prometheus
Bearded adult Spartan
Zeus
Eagle

▲ HEROES

During the archaic period, Sparta was like other *poleis*, producing fine poets and artists who made beautiful painted pottery. This Spartan cup shows the legendary hero, Prometheus, who brought fire to humanity – a godlike deed that went against Zeus's wishes. For acting in this way, Zeus condemned Prometheus to have his organs pecked out by an eagle.

▲ HUNTING

Spartan citizens belonged to dining clubs where they shared simple meals with fellow members. Each Spartan was expected to provide food for the dining clubs from their landholdings and by hunting wild animals, such as boar, with spears. This was another way of training for war, as the painting on this cup shows.

▲ NO MORE ART

In the 7th century BC, Spartan life changed completely when the Messenians rebelled, and almost overthrew their masters. Fear of further rebellions made the Spartans give up fine arts to devote themselves completely to war. As a result, they no longer made beautiful drinking cups like this, which shows Zeus and his sacred eagle.

Long, styled hair

◄ LONG-HAIRED WARRIORS

The Spartans did not look like other Greeks. Male citizens dressed alike, in scarlet cloaks, and wore their hair long. They took great pride over this hair, which they always carefully combed before battle. There was a Spartan saying that long hair made handsome men better looking, and ugly ones more terrifying. This bronze figure is a long-haired Spartan warrior wrapped tightly in his cloak.

Young warrior with spear

SPARTAN SIMPLICITY ►

Spartans did not believe in displays of wealth and luxury, and did not even mint coins – they used heavy iron bars instead. Their speech was also simple and direct, using as few words as possible. Our word "laconic" (of few words) originates from Laconia, the Spartan homeland.

Ploughman
Ox

◄ HELOTS

Spartan citizens were greatly outnumbered by free non-Spartans and "helots" – the original inhabitants of Laconia and neighbouring Messenia, whom the Spartans had enslaved. Unlike other slaves, helots did not belong to individuals. They were the collective property of the state, which assigned them to work on farmland for individual Spartans. The Spartans' greatest fear was that the helots would rebel, as they did in 464 BC.

GROWING UP IN SPARTA

Spartan education and child rearing were controlled by the state. This was not the case in other Greek *poleis*. The Spartans wanted to produce tough, disciplined soldiers, and needed strong, healthy women who could give birth to more soldiers, thus creating Greece's most powerful army. Training began early. Except for heirs to the kingship, all Spartan boys went through brutal challenges to make them fearless warriors.

Baby held by mother

Tunic

Sparta

◄ SPARTAN BABIES

Every baby born to a Spartan citizen was shown to a council of elders at a meeting place called a *lesche*. The elders assessed each baby's strength and decided whether it deserved to live or die. Deformed or sickly babies were taken to a steep cliff to the west of Sparta and left to die. Healthy babies had to learn to be tough. Spartan mothers trained children to be able to spend time alone and in the dark, and not to cry or be fussy about their food.

▲ SPARTAN GIRLS

In most Greek *poleis*, girls had little physical exercise, spending much of their time sitting as they spun and wove wool. In Sparta, however, spinning and weaving were left to slave women. Spartan girls, like the one shown in this 6th-century bronze figurine, had to go through hard physical training to turn them into strong, healthy women.

▲ TOUGHENING UP

At age seven, boys were sent to live in a barracks overseen by a *paidonomos* ("controller of boys") whose job was to harden them up. They were underfed and thinly clothed to get them used to hunger and cold. This 1860s painting by Edgar Degas shows Spartan boys preparing to wrestle.

▲ PHYSICAL EXERCISE

During training, boys lived in *boua* ("herds"). The captain of the troop was the boy who showed the best judgement and strongest fighting spirit. They were taught only basic reading and writing. Boys spent most of their days doing physical exercise, such as running and throwing the discus.

SPARTAN LEGACY

Spartan education was an inspiration to the founders of British public schools, such as Eton, in the 18th century. It was thought that cold showers, cold dormitories, early rising, and physical exercise were good for children. Such schools taught a code of discipline, duty, and self-sacrifice, and schoolboys were whipped for bad behaviour. In the Eton wall game (*above*), one pupil even died. Life was harder still for Spartan boys, who were also whipped purely to see how much pain they could endure. The fact that Spartans all went through the same harsh upbringing created a sense of unity and equality between them.

JOINING A DINING CLUB ▲

At the age of 20 a Spartan was eligible to join a *pheidition* ("dining club"). To keep existing members of the club happy, each applicant had to be accepted by every member of the club. They voted using balls of bread which they tossed into a bowl – a crushed ball meant that the applicant was rejected. Membership of a dining club was a requirement of Spartan citizenship.

Warrior fighting a snake

MILITARY TRAINING ►

Young Spartan men practised mock battles, learned to fight with a sword and a lance, and to march in tight ranks, shoulder to shoulder. Music was also part of the military education, and the Spartans played pipes and sang songs as they marched into battle. Youths in military training were watched by elders, who encouraged them to fight well.

Bare feet

▲ TOUGH MOTHERS

Women were supposed to pass on Spartan values. In wartime, a mother gave her son a shield (as in this painting by the French artist Jean-Jacques Lagrenée), stating that he should return carrying the shield – or lying dead upon it. Mothers were meant to rejoice if their sons died in battle.

DETAIL OF A SPARTAN
CUP FROM THE
6TH CENTURY BC

GROWING UP IN ATHENS

In Athens, poorer children only had a basic education before being sent out to work as soon as they were old enough to help their parents. Poorer boys often followed the trade of their father, working alongside him in the family workshop. For richer boys, there were schools which taught reading, writing, arithmetic, literature, and music. Life was very different for girls, who were usually taught at home by their mothers or slaves. They learned to read and write, to spin and weave wool, to store supplies and prepare meals and often to play musical instruments.

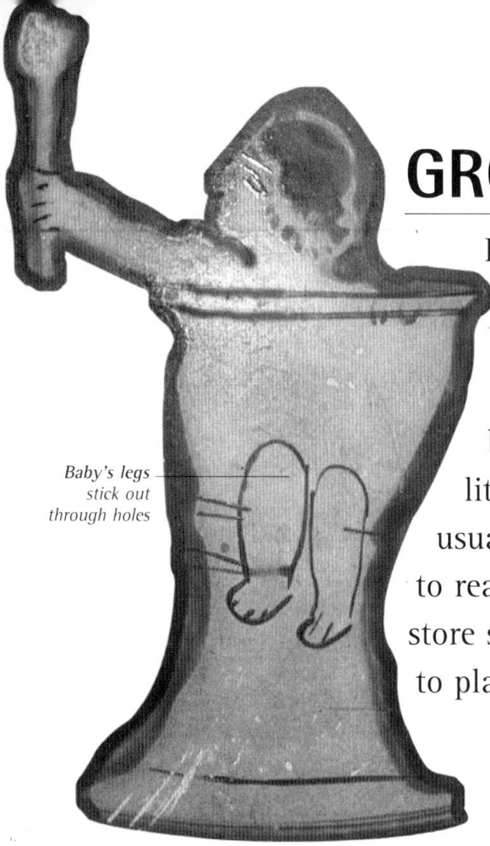

Baby's legs stick out through holes

▲ BABIES
Boys and girls spent their earliest years at home with their mothers. This vase painting shows a baby with a rattle sitting in a large pot. This stopped the baby crawling off into danger and also served as a potty. Pots like this have been found by archaeologists in Athens.

Athens

Braided hair

TOYS ▶
Children who died were often buried with their favourite toys. Various toys have been found in graves, such as these two riders – one on a horse and one on a goose. Archaeologists have also discovered dolls and animals, which could be pulled along on wheels.

Painted terracotta

▼ SCHOOL
Boys were taught at the teacher's home. They were accompanied by a *paidagogos*, a family slave who was responsible for the boy's behaviour. This vase shows a music and literature lesson. On the left, the boy and teacher practise the lyre. On the right, the boy stands in front of the teacher to recite a poem about the Trojan War.

Basket

Scroll

LITERATURE LESSONS

Wax tablet

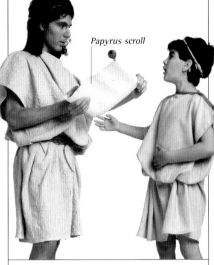

Papyrus scroll

WRITING
Since writing paper was expensive, boys and girls learned to write with a pointed piece of wood or metal on a wooden tablet coated with wax. This pottery figurine depicts someone writing on a tablet, which could be smoothed over and reused. Writing paper for letters and books was made from papyrus leaves imported from Egypt.

POETRY LESSONS
Pupils learned poems by heart, particularly the writings of Homer. The Greeks thought that Homer was a great teacher of morals (good behaviour) to the young, and the poet's works were often quoted by adult Athenians in speeches and conversations. This boy is reciting some lines from Homer for his teacher.

MILITARY TRAINING ▲
Older boys practised using weapons so they could later serve Athens as soldiers. Unlike in Sparta, there was no formal military training until the 4th century BC, when Athenians were expected to go through a two-year period of instruction in handling weapons. This teaching took place in barracks in Piraeus, the port of Athens.

Paidagogos watches the lesson

Youths running a race

▲ PHYSICAL EXERCISE
Boys spent a lot of their time in the *palaestra* (wrestling ground) or gymnasium. They played competitive games under the eye of a trainer called a *paidotribes*. Games included running, long jump, wrestling, boxing, and throwing the javelin and discus. The *paidotribes* also taught dancing so that boys could take part in dances during religious festivals. This was also another good way of keeping fit, and fitness was always encouraged because the *polis* depended on the strength of its citizen-soldiers to survive.

SOPHISTS

Education for young men was provided by travelling "sophists" ("experts" or "wise men"). For a fee, they taught a wide variety of subjects, including science, philosophy, and rhetoric – the art of persuasive public speaking. This statue shows Athens' greatest orator (speechmaker), Demosthenes (384–322 BC). He was taught by an older orator called Isaeus, and Demosthenes, in turn, gave lessons to younger pupils.

Kithara

MUSIC

Singing, playing instruments, and dancing were enjoyed everywhere in Greece, and music played its part in every area of life. Religious hymns were sung in worship, while the *aulos*, a kind of pipe, was played on battleships (so that the rowers could keep time), and also to accompany soldiers marching into war. After a victory, the winning side sang *paeans* – songs of thanksgiving or triumph. Men also sang *paeans* to the gods at their wine-drinking parties.

Lyre held between thighs

MUSIC LESSONS ▶
Lyre teachers, or *kitharistes*, taught from home. Musical accomplishment was seen to be character-building, but only rich, upper-class families could afford the lessons. The philosopher Plato wrote that music masters "instil self-control and deter the young from evil-doing . . . By this means, they become more civilized, more balanced, and better adjusted."

music

▲ DIVINE MUSIC
The Greeks believed that music had special powers, including healing the sick. In Greek myth, the musician Orpheus played so beautifully that wild animals came to hear him play, peacefully lying down at his feet. Here he plucks a *kithara*, a large lyre with a hollow body made from wood or ivory. It was said to have been invented by Apollo, god of music.

Aulos (double pipe)

Trigonon (harp)

THE MUSES ▶
Our word "music" comes from the Greek word *mousike* – the art of the muses. The muses were the goddesses who inspired all musicians and poets. The nine muses – Calliope, Clio, Erato, Euterpe, Melpomene, Polyhymnia, Terpsichore, Thalia, and Urania – were thought to live on Mount Olympus, singing continually in sweet harmonious voices, to the delight of the other gods. The muses can be seen here playing instruments, including two *auloi*.

MUSICAL INSTRUMENTS

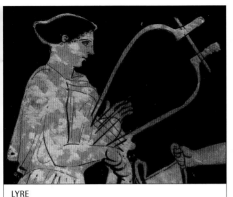

LYRE
In Greek myth, the first lyre was made by the god Hermes from a tortoise shell and the horns and hide of an ox, stolen from his brother, Apollo. This lyre has a sounding box made from a tortoise shell and wooden arms. Like guitars now, lyres were plucked with the fingers or struck with a plectrum – a small, thin piece of metal, bone, or similar material.

AULOS
The *aulos* was a pair of pipes played like an oboe, by blowing across a vibrating reed in each mouthpiece. Each pipe had several sound holes like a recorder. Its sound was more piercing and stirring than other instruments, and the *aulos* was played to accompany such events as religious processions, men's drinking sessions, and lively dances.

SYRINX
The Greeks thought the *syrinx*, or pan-pipes, were invented by the god Pan (*above*), the god of the countryside. Country people, such as shepherds, played the instrument. The *syrinx* had several pipes tied together, and was played by blowing across the ends of each one. The pipes were plugged with wax at varying lengths to create a range of notes.

◄ APOLLO
Apollo, god of music, was proud of his skill at playing the lyre. According to myth, he took part in a musical contest with Pan, judged by King Midas of Phrygia (in modern Turkey). When Midas said that he preferred Pan's pipe playing, Apollo became so angry that he gave Midas a pair of donkey's ears for his decision. Another myth told of Apollo's contest with Marsyas, a satyr who played the *aulos* so well that listeners said that not even Apollo could play better. Marsyas did not deny this, so Apollo challenged him to a competition, which Apollo won by playing his lyre upside down. Apollo skinned Marsyas alive for challenging a god.

Dancing satyr

Kithara

Lyre

Aulos

▲ DANCING
The Greeks loved to dance. They thought dancing, like music, was invented by the gods. Most religious festivals included dances. People also danced to celebrate victories in war, weddings, the naming of infants, and the end of a harvest. In his *Iliad*, Homer describes young men and girls dancing together, hand in hand, while "around the lovely chorus of dancers stood a great crowd, happily watching". Traditional dances still play a very important role in Greek life.

AT HOME

Greek houses were designed to be private and secure. The outer windows were small, and living areas were not visible from the street. Light came into the house from an open courtyard, which connected the surrounding rooms. There was often an upper floor, reached by a ladder or stairs. The walls were made from mud bricks or rubble with wood frames, sometimes on a stone base. Unlike the stone walls of temples, mud brick and rubble walls have not survived, so archaeologists work out the layouts of houses from the bases of the walls. They can guess what rooms were used for by their size and position.

▲ POTTERY
Pottery was the most common item in Greek houses. It has survived long after the mud bricks and wooden furniture crumbled to dust. The discovery of a large number of pots in a single room suggests it was used to store foods such as wine, oil, or olives.

VASE PAINTINGS ▲
Vase paintings, such as this one of a woman sitting on a chair, show us what Greek furniture looked like. Furniture, including couches, small tables, and chairs, was light and portable so that it could be moved from room to room easily.

Windows overlooking courtyard

Pottery tiles

Tiny windows to prevent thieves breaking in

Stone base of walls

Doorway

▲ GREEK HOUSES
This is an artist's impression of a house in Athens. The home it is based on was discovered south-east of the *agora* and was the home and workshop of Micion, a sculptor. Micion lived here in about 470 BC. The doorway leads into the courtyard, with rooms on three sides. You can see the stone foundations of the mud-brick walls – the only part of the house that has survived.

▲ OLYNTHUS FLOORS
This artwork shows the *andron* ("men's room"), of a house in Olynthus (in Thrace), where the owner held parties for his friends. Its floor had a pebble mosaic. One of the few areas shown to outsiders, the *andron* was the most richly decorated room in the house.

◄ STORAGE

There were no cupboards or shelves in Greek houses. Instead, clothes and other goods were stored in wooden chests, like the one shown in this relief. The Athenian Xenophon explained how different parts of the house were chosen to store different goods: "The most private and strongest room in the house seems to demand the money, jewels, and valuables; the dry places expect the corn; the coolest parts are the most convenient for the wine."

Box resting on deep chest

Wooden chair

COOKING

COOKING AT THE HEARTH

Women often cooked over the open fire in the hearth. They used a large pot that rested on a grid or on a three-legged stand made of bronze. This was called a tripod, as shown in this pottery model. The pots were usually made out of fired clay, although richer families might also have pots made of bronze.

PORTABLE COOKERS

Greek women sometimes used portable cookers. These were pots in which charcoal was burned to heat up other pots. Food could also be held over the pot and cooked on spits. Portable cookers, like the one in this terracotta model, allowed women to prepare meals in other parts of the house, such as the courtyard.

homes

WASHING ►

Greek houses did not have their own supply of running water. Water was collected in jars every day from a public fountain, then brought home so the family could wash. Water was heated at the hearth and poured into a pottery washbasin or a small hip bath, also made of pottery. Toilets were simple – a wooden seat over a pottery bucket, which was emptied into the street.

Athlete washing at basin

HEARTH ►

Hestia was the goddess of the hearth, or fireplace, which was at the centre of every Greek home. At the start of each meal, an offering of food was thrown onto the fire for the goddess. A newborn baby was always carried around the hearth, and brides and new slaves were also brought there to be welcomed into the family. The hearth was used to cook food, heat water, and also warm the home on winter evenings.

RELIEF FROM A
MOTHER'S TOMBSTONE

WOMEN'S LIVES

Most of our information about Greek women's lives comes from writings by upper-class Athenian men, who thought that a woman's place was in the home. Yet even in Athens, where women had less freedom than in other *poleis*, they did not spend all their lives indoors. They worked as midwives, wet nurses, and small-scale market traders. Upper-class women played public roles, as priestesses serving goddesses. In the countryside, poor women worked in the fields with their husbands. Women of all classes took part in religious festivals.

WOMEN'S FESTIVAL ▲

The *Thesmophoria* was an autumn festival in honour of Demeter, goddess of the fields. It was celebrated all over Greece by women alone to ensure a good harvest the following year. In Athens, women left their husbands for three days to camp in the hillside sanctuary of Demeter. They offered piglets as a sacrifice, and threw them into a pit. What else took place is unknown because men were forbidden to attend, and women kept the rites secret.

women's
lives

◄ MOTHERHOOD

Men took the view that the purpose of marriage was to raise male heirs to inherit property and carry on the family line. Babies were born at home, and the birth was overseen by women – either members of the family or professional midwives. In Euripides' tragedy *Medea*, the heroine compares the bravery of men in war with that of mothers, who endure the pain of childbirth. She declares, "I'd rather face the battle line three times than go through childbirth once." Spartan women who died in childbirth were honoured in a similar way to men who died in battle – their names were carved on their tombstones, and they may have been given public funerals. This marble relief shows a mother gazing lovingly at her baby.

Woollen garment

Weights

CHILDHOOD

Young girls stayed at home with their mothers, who taught them how to spin, weave, and cook, to prepare them for their main goal in life – marriage. A woman called Procne, in a play by Sophocles, says, "As little girls, we live the sweetest life of all human beings in our father's house . . . But once we reach the age of reason, we are thrust outside . . . some to good homes, others to abusive ones. And we have to praise such things and think that everything is fine."

MARRIAGE

Marriage was a business arrangement in which a girl's father, brother, or male guardian gave her away to another man – whether she wanted this or not. Girls married young, between the ages of 12 and 15, to much older husbands. This age difference may have enabled a husband to shape his wife's character and to control her behaviour. This painting shows women in a wedding procession. Water from a special spring is being carried in a tall vase for the bride's ritual bath.

WOMEN'S WORK

In the home, an important job for a woman was to spin wool and weave it into cloth on an upright loom that rested against the wall. Vertical "warp" threads were fixed to the top of the loom, with weights tied at the bottom. Another thread, the "weft", was passed in between the warps, from one side to the other. All clothes were made this way, and even rich Greek women spun and wove. Weaving was both creative and useful, so women were praised for it.

Grinding grain to make flour for bread

SAPPHO

Several Greek women were well-known poets. One of the greatest was Sappho, who lived on the island of Lesbos in the 6th century BC. There were already nine muses of the arts, and Sappho was so popular that she was called the "tenth muse". She was also headmistress of a school for girls, and sometimes wrote about her students in her poetry.

Pot balanced on woman's head

AT THE FOUNTAIN ▶

It was a woman's duty to fetch water every morning from a public fountain – a place to meet friends and chat. Aristophanes' comedy *Lysistrata* includes a chorus of women carrying water pots. They complain, "At dawn, I filled my water jar from the fountain with difficulty in the middle of a crowd, noise, and the clattering of pots, jostled by slave women." This painting comes from a vase which was itself used to collect water.

THE SYMPOSIUM

The favourite leisure activity of Greek men was a dinner party. The man of the house invited male friends to his home, where they ate and drank, reclining on couches. The evening was divided into two parts – *deipnon* ("meal") and *symposion* ("drinking together") – now more commonly known by the Latin word *symposium*. The occasion followed formal rules.

Guest leaning on his left elbow and eating with his right hand

THE ANDRON ▶
A slave met guests at the door, then washed their hands and feet, and showed them to the *andron* (men's room). They reclined on couches, often two sharing a single couch. The comic writer Aristophanes explained how to behave at a fashionable drinking party: "Recline graciously . . . Pour yourself back into the cushions with a supple athletic grace . . . Now you should say something complimentary about the bronze ornaments."

Cup showing an actor in a padded costume

▲ PARASITES
It was common for people to gatecrash parties. Men who regularly came uninvited were known as parasites – literally meaning "beside the food". Like jesters, they earned a meal by flattering the host, telling jokes, and allowing themselves to be made fun of by other guests. Our word "parasite", meaning a creature (such as a flea) which lives off another creature, derives from the ancient Greek for "gatecrasher". Parasites often appear in Greek comedies.

◀ THE MEAL
The first part of the evening was taken up with the *deipnon*, when various dishes were served by slaves. The food was placed on small tables, like those being carried by the man and woman in this vase painting. Dishes were usually simple, such as bean soup, cheese, olives, fish grilled over an open fire, or pork sausages. Pork was the most commonly available meat. While the guests were eating they did not drink, preferring to keep the two separate. The wine was brought out later.

LIBATIONS AND A HYMN ▶
After the meal, guests washed their hands and were given a cup of wine. Usually Greeks diluted wine with water – and Hesiod recommended that dilution should be three parts water to one part wine. However, for a libation (an offering to the gods), wine was drunk undiluted. Having almost drained their cups, they poured the remainder onto the ground as an offering. They then sang a hymn to Dionysus, the god of wine.

Dionysus, with vines in the background

Centaurs fighting Greeks

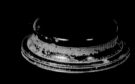
symposium

Aulos (pipe) player

SYMPOSIARCH ▶
The drinking session also followed a fairly strict plan. A *symposiarch*, or master of ceremonies, was chosen, sometimes by throwing dice. He decided the strength of the wine, which was mixed with water in a large deep vessel called a *krater* (*right*), and then served in cups by slave boys or women. He might also choose a subject for discussion, such as love or philosophy.

◀ ENTERTAINMENT
Wealthy hosts provided acrobats, musicians, and dancers as entertainment. Plato disapproved: "When the company are real gentlemen and men of education, you will see no flute girls nor dancing girls nor harp girls; they will have no nonsense nor games, but will be content with one another's conversation."

▲ GAMES AND SONGS
Guests also made their own entertainment, singing traditional and often rude drinking songs called *skolia*. There was also a popular game called *kottabos* ("wine throw") in which guests flicked drops of wine at a target, such as cups floating in water (*above*). The writer Athenaeus said that some took as much pride in winning at *kottabos* as others did in throwing the javelin.

Man looks over his shoulder at the youth behind him

Aulos

END OF THE EVENING ▶
The evening often ended with drunkenness, dancing, and a *komos* – a rowdy procession through the streets. This was the time when drunk young men often misbehaved. The historian Thucydides wrote that in Athens statues were "defaced by young men who were enjoying themselves after having too much drink". This vase painting shows a wild *komos* led by a slave girl.

*Athlete
holds strigil*

THE GYMNASIUM

The Greeks built *gymnasia* for the military and athletic training of *ephebes* – men aged 18 to 20. *Gymnasia* were also used by older athletes training for sporting festivals, and by other citizens, who went there to meet friends, exercise, and bathe. This was a public institution, freely available to every adult male. Each gymnasium had a *palaestra* ("wrestling ground") and a running track, as well as shaded walks, gardens, baths, changing rooms, and altars to the gods.

◄ WRESTLING
Every day the *palaestra* was filled with pairs of youths wrestling. They used a wide variety of holds and throws, which their trainers helped them to master. The wrestler tried to throw his opponent so that his knees touched the ground. It usually took three throws to win a contest. It was hard to get a grip, because the wrestlers' bodies were slippery with olive oil. This cup painting shows a successful throw – the lower wrestler has lost his balance and is falling, with his left knee about to touch the ground.

gymnasium

◄ BODY BEAUTIFUL
The gymnasium provided yet another opportunity for Greek men to compete with each other. They competed not just to win at wrestling matches, but also to have the most perfect bodies. Physical beauty was of great importance to Greek men, who were surrounded by sculptures and paintings of perfectly proportioned males with muscular, toned bodies.

ACADEMY ▲
In Athens, *gymnasia* were also centres of learning, where Greeks could hear lectures on various subjects. The philosopher Plato taught in an Athenian gymnasium called the Academy, named after a local hero, Academos. Around the world there are now many "academies", which promote the arts and sciences. This is the National Academy of Athens, built in 1859-87.

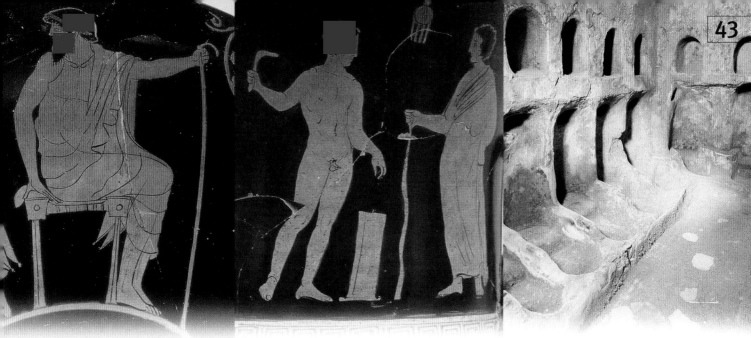

▲ GYMNASIARCHS

Gymnasia were run and paid for by officials called *gymnasiarchs*, who were selected from the wealthier citizens. They needed to have enough money to pay for the olive oil given to the athletes, and for the fuel used to heat bath water. Serving as a *gymnasiarch* was an honour. The role worked like a tax on rich people, channelling their wealth into something for the good of everyone.

▲ OIL AND STRIGIL

Before exercising, Greeks rubbed their bodies with olive oil and dust. This helped to keep them warm, and also prevented wrestling opponents from getting a firm grip on them. After exercising, they scraped away the oil and dirt with a bronze tool called a strigil. Youths in training were often scraped clean by masseurs called *aleiptes*, who might also give them a massage to relax their muscles.

▲ BATHS

A gymnasium usually included a bathhouse, with rows of terracotta hip baths, sunk into the ground. The bathers sat side by side in water that had been heated by slaves. Bathhouses were often circular buildings, allowing bathers to chat to each other across the room. Most Greeks did not have their own baths at home, so they used those at the gymnasium.

Open space for wrestling

Corinthian columns supported roofed walkway

◀ PALAESTRA

The *palaestra* was an enclosed square courtyard. It was surrounded by porticoes – double rows of columns supporting a roof that provided shade from the sun and shelter from the rain. The *palaestra* was usually built alongside a larger courtyard where athletes practised other sports, such as throwing the discus and the javelin, and long jumping. This larger courtyard was called the gymnasium, although the name also referred to the whole complex of buildings.

Chlamys *is fastened on the right shoulder*

CLOTHES

Unlike the clothes we wear today, Greek clothing was not cut to fit. Garments were made up of rectangles of woollen or linen cloth, woven by women on a loom at home. The entire piece of cloth was worn either as a cloak draped around the body or as a tunic. These clothes were easy to clean and store – they were simply folded and placed in chests. Greeks thought that close-fitting or tailored garments, such as trousers, were the clothing of barbarians.

HEPHAESTUS, GOD OF METALWORKERS

WORK CLOTHES ▶

Men who did manual work, such as farmers, craftsmen, and slaves, wore a short tunic, called an *exomis*. This was fastened over the left shoulder while the right arm and chest were exposed. It was a practical outfit that allowed the arms and legs to move freely.

◀ SHAVING

Until the late 4th century BC, adult Greek men grew beards. It was only when Alexander the Great continu[ed] to shave into adulthood – and encouraged his soldiers to do the same – that the fashion for shaving began. Alexander claimed this would prevent enemies seizing soldiers by their beards in battle.

HIMATION ▶

The main garment worn by men of the middle and upper classes was the *himation* – a rectangle of woollen cloth, measuring approximately 2.8 x 1.75 m (9 x 6 ft), which could be draped around the body in various ways. Upper-class Athenians often covered both arms with their *himation*, a style indicating that they did not have to work for a living, and had a slave to dress them. This statue of Sophocles shows how the *himation* could be worn in an elegant manner.

◀ YOUTHFUL DRESS

The Greeks thought the late teenage years were an important stage in a boy's path to manhood. *Ephebes*, young men aged 18 to 20, were clean shaven and often wore a short cloak called a *chlamys*. The *chlamys* was also worn by soldiers, particularly horsemen.

clothes

JEWELLERY

NECKLACE
Women from rich families displayed their wealth and taste with elaborate jewellery. After death, they were buried with their jewellery and a large amount of it has been found in graves dating back to Minoan times. This gold pendant in the shape of a pair of bees was found on Crete, in the Minoan palace of Malia.

EARRINGS
This pair of highly detailed gold earrings shows the heads of griffins. Griffins were mythical creatures – part-eagle and part-lion – which first appear in Minoan and Mycenaean art. The Greeks believed that griffins lived in Scythia, north of the Black Sea, where they guarded the gold mines.

BRACELET
There were many types of bracelet, worn on the arms and legs. This one has two gold lion heads. In one comedy, Aristophanes described the jewellery worn by one woman: " . . . earrings, a pendant . . . pins, necklet, armlet, bangles, collars of jewels, anklets, chains, rings . . . It's past man's power to tell you all the things."

RING
Men as well as women wore rings. They were often set with precious and semiprecious stones or coloured glass. The glass was sometimes engraved with a picture, which could be pushed into soft wax to sign a document. This ring shows a seated figure with a dog. Only a very skilled craftsman could carve such a tiny image.

▼ COSMETICS
Women had a wide variety of perfumes and cosmetics, including red colouring for the lips, and black for the eyebrows and eyelashes. Make-up was stored in small jars called *aryballoi*. Like other Greek vases, *aryballoi* were often decorated with scenes displaying what they were used for. This one is painted with women getting dressed.

Wall decoration

Himations, draped like those of men

Basket of wool

◄ CHITON
Women wore a long tunic called a *chiton*. This came in two different styles – the Doric *chiton*, developed by mainland Greeks, and the Ionic *chiton*, created in Ionia. A Doric *chiton* was made of two narrow rectangles of cloth, and was sleeveless. This woman wears the much wider Ionic *chiton*, where extra material was used to form sleeves.

Umbrella-like cover protects statue

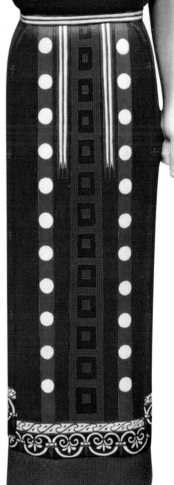

Embroidery

PEPLOS ►
Until the 4th century BC, Greek women wore a *peplos* on top of their *chiton*. This was a belted robe with a fold at the top which reached down to the waist. Traces of paint on statues show that the *peplos* was often brightly coloured. This cast of a statue of a young woman has been painted to show the original colours of her *peplos*, worn over a blue *chiton*.

Veil worn in public

Fastening pins at shoulders

◄ DORIC CHITON
This statue shows a woman wearing the sleeveless Doric *chiton*. Like the *peplos*, this was formed by two long rectangles of cloth. In the 4th century BC, many women stopped wearing a *peplos* over their tunic, replacing it with the *himation*, like those worn by men.

SLAVES

The population of every Greek *polis* included large numbers of slaves – people who were bought and sold in the marketplace as property. Many slaves were of foreign origin – from lands around the Black Sea, the Balkans, and the Middle East. Aristotle thought that, unlike the Greeks, all barbarians were slaves by nature. However, the Greeks also enslaved their fellow Greeks after wars. Life for a slave varied depending on the kind of work he or she did.

▲ SLAVES OF WAR
In 416 BC, the Athenians conquered the island of Melos, killed all the men, and sold the women and children into slavery. Even some Athenians found this shocking. Soon after, the playwright Euripides wrote an antiwar play called *The Trojan Women* to show the suffering of women who became slaves.

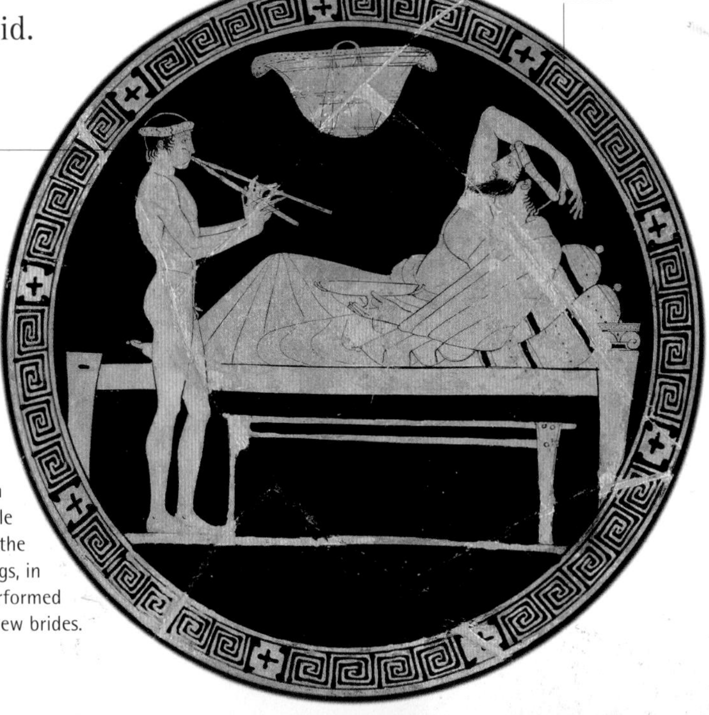

SCYTHIAN ARCHER

Master

Slave boy plays an aulos

HOUSEHOLD SLAVES ▶
Every well-off Greek family owned male and female slaves. They lived in the house and were often treated as members of the family. A slave in a play by Euripides says, "It's low not to feel with your masters, laugh with them, and sympathize in their sorrows." New female slaves were welcomed into the household with nuts and figs, in the ritual that was also performed to welcome new brides.

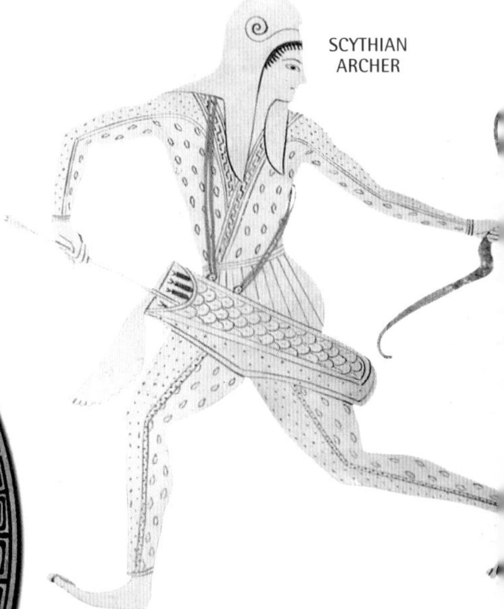

▲ PUBLIC SERVANTS
In Athens, many public servants were slaves owned by the *polis*. These included Scythian bowmen, who acted as a police force, the officials who checked the weights and measures used by marketplace traders, and the clerks who kept records of trials in the law courts. These public slaves lived more comfortably than many poor Athenian citizens.

Slave driving a plough

Oxen

Mined silver in its rough form

▲ SLAVE POPULATIONS

Greek invaders conquered and enslaved local populations in Sparta, Thessaly, Crete, Syracuse, and Heraclea on the Black Sea, and forced them to work as farmers. In Sparta, Thessaly, and Crete, these slaves were Greek, just like their owners. These slaves were owned as a single group, rather than as individuals, as was usually the case. They had certain rights, such as being allowed to marry and raise families.

slaves

SILVER MINES ▲

Athens owned between 10,000 and 40,000 slaves, mostly prisoners of war and convicted criminals, who worked in the state silver mines at Laureion. Conditions were extremely harsh, and the slaves did not survive for many years. After digging out the raw material, slaves crushed, washed, and heated it to separate the pure silver from other materials.

SLAVE BUSINESSES ▼

In Athens, many privately owned slaves worked alongside their owners in craft workshops, as potters, shoemakers, or sculptors. Some were hired out to work for other people while others ran their own businesses, giving a share of their profits to their owners. They could save money, and would eventually be able to buy their freedom. During the 4th century BC, one of the richest men in Athens was an ex-slave called Pasion, who was both a banker and the owner of a shield factory, where he employed his own slaves.

Statue completed by sculptor

INSIDE THE SILVER MINES

MINING SILVER
To get at the silver at Laureion, slaves had to tunnel underground, following the veins of silver embedded in the rock. Using picks, shovels, hammers, and chisels, they dug galleries and deep shafts wide enough to creep inside and remove the metal. Because wood was in short supply, pillars of rock were left to support the roof.

LIGHTING
Archaeologists at Laureion have found tools left by miners and also the tiny pottery oil lamps the slaves used to find their way around the dark galleries. Each lamp provided only a small amount of light, so the miners had to get used to working in almost total darkness.

ON THE SURFACE
The veins of silver did not contain pure metal but a mixture of silver and rock, called ore. The slaves hacked out lumps of the ore from the surrounding rocks, then loaded it into baskets to bring to the surface. Once the ore had been brought out of the mine, the slaves' next job was to crush it with heavy hammers.

WASHING THE ORE
The slaves placed the crushed ore in a washery – a raised stone channel with water flowing through grooves cut inside it. The water carried away the lighter rock while the heavier metals, including the silver, sank to the bottom and were trapped in the hollows seen here. The silver was then scooped out by slaves.

FARMING

Greece has a hot, Mediterranean climate, and is a land of wooded mountains, scrub-covered hills, and fertile valleys. The plains in the valleys were the only places where cereal crops (mainly barley) could be grown. Even here, the soil was often thin and dotted with rocks, which made the farmer's life difficult. The comic playwright, Menander, describes the hardship of a typical Athenian farmer "struggling with rocks that yield nothing but savory and sage, and getting nothing out of it but aches and pains".

◄ OLIVES

The olive was the most important Greek crop, for it was one of the few trees able to produce fruit in dry and rocky conditions. Olives were very useful, both for food, and for their oil, which was used for cooking, lighting, and as a cosmetic. Olives were so important to the Athenians that they believed olive trees were a gift from the goddess Athena, specially created for their dry soil. Like vines, they were grown on hillsides on flat terraces, which Greek farmers built by heaping up earth behind stone walls.

COWLAND

Unlike the dry and rocky land in Attica, Boeotia in central Greece had a wide fertile plain with good soil for growing grain and pasture (grassland). Boeotia means "cowland" because, unlike most Greeks, the farmers here raised large herds of cattle. This was the home of the poet Hesiod, whose *Works and Days* offered advice about how to run a farm, using the movement of the stars as a calendar. Like other ancient peoples, the Greeks recognized star constellation patterns during different times of the year and gave them names that we still use.

ANIMALS

GOAT
Goats were common because of their hardiness and ability to eat almost anything – even thorny plants. Like sheep, they provided farmers with milk (which was made into cheese) and meat. In summer, goats were driven up into the mountains and watched over by goatherds, who brought them down to the valleys in winter for protection. In summer, goatherding was a full-time job, separate from other farming work.

SHEEP
Every Greek home needed wool for making clothes, and farmers could always sell wool in the local market. The Greeks drank sheep and goat's milk much more than cow's milk. It was what they were used to, since many people owned goats and sheep, but few owned cows. Some doctors even claimed that cow's milk was unhealthy. The Greeks still use goat and sheep milk to make feta cheese and yoghurt.

DONKEY
As they do today, farmers in ancient Greece used donkeys for transport, to carry harvested crops home from the fields, and also for taking goods to market. Horses were only owned by rich people, because they had to be fed on grain to stay in good condition. Donkeys could live on grass and weeds alone. These ceremonial drinking cups, decorated with animals' heads, are known as *rhytons*.

PIG
Pigs were easy for farmers to keep because they ate almost anything, and could be fed on acorns and beech nuts in autumn. This meant that even the poorest Greek farmers could keep pigs. Pork was eaten more often than any other meat. As well as pork sausages, the Greeks also ate black puddings made from pigs' blood. The animals were smaller and hairier than the pigs we see today.

PLOUGHING TIME ▶
The farmer's work ran in cycles, with periods of hard work when ploughing, sowing, and harvesting was needed. Ploughing was done in autumn and in spring, using oxen. The plough was a wooden wedge, tipped with iron, used to cut a furrow through the soil. This was fastened to a beam, attached to the oxen by a yoke or crossbar. Farmers made their own ploughs.

Yoke

GRAPES ▶
After olives, grapes were the second most important crop for the Greeks, due to the huge popularity of wine. Vines needed more care than olive groves, because they had to be pruned and trained. This vase painting shows the harvesting of grapes. The branches of the vines are trailing on long poles stuck into the ground. Grapes were picked by hand.

Triptolemos

Bag of corn

farming

Demeter

Winged chariot

◀ FARMING GODS
Farming was always risky – crops could be destroyed by drought, pests, or invading armies in wartime. Farmers were very religious, offering prayer and sacrifices to gods such as Demeter (the grain goddess) in the hope that their hard work would not be wasted. The Greeks believed that Demeter first taught people how to farm. She gave corn to the hero, Triptolemos, and sent him off in a winged chariot to spread the knowledge of farming around the world.

SEA TRADERS

No Greek city was far from the coast, so trade was usually carried out by sea. Greek merchant ships moved slowly and carried small crews, so were were often attacked by pirates who travelled around the Mediterranean. Another risk was of being shipwrecked, either by sailing into hidden rocks or being caught in sudden storms. More than 1,000 ancient shipwrecks have been found throughout the Mediterranean (dating from the 8th century BC onwards), often after divers spotted pots and other relics scattered on the sea bed. These have helped archaeologists to learn some remarkable facts about the ancient Greeks.

▲ THE WINDS

Ships with square sails could not sail directly into the wind, so sailors had to wait for the wind to blow in the right direction before setting off. The winds were worshipped as gods with their own names and personalities. The main wind gods were Boreas (north), Zephyrus (west), Notus (south), and Eurus (east). Boreas was a violent wind, bringing icy gales in winter, which stopped ships from sailing. In art, he was represented as a winged, bearded man. Zephyrus was a gentle wind, a winged youth with sweet breath. This mosaic shows one of the winds, perhaps Boreas. His head rises out of the sea, with a shell beside it.

sea traders

GOODS

GREEN OLIVES

ALMONDS

Many different goods were traded all around the Mediterranean. The Athenian poet, Hermippus described just a few of the products the ships carried: "From Cyrene stalks of silphium and hides of oxen, from the Hellespont mackerel and salted fish . . . from Egypt, rigging for sails and papyrus, from Syria frankincense, from glorious Crete cypress . . . from the Paphlagonians, glossy almonds."

Pyrenees

Empor

IBERIA

Silver
Gold
Copper
Hemeroscopium
Wi
Balear
Island
Gades Mainaca

Lixus

Square sail

Mast

◄ TRADING SHIP

This painting on a cup shows a typical merchant ship. It is powered by a single square sail and steered by a pair of oars at the stern. At the rear is a small ladder for climbing on and off the ship. The sail has been rolled up. This was done in windy weather to prevent it from tearing. The ship carried a small crew and could sail for many days without docking. The Greeks painted eyes on the bows for good luck – they thought this allowed the ship to see dangers ahead. This custom is continued by Greek fishermen today.

▲ COINS

Early Greek traders bartered (exchanged) goods. They could only obtain products if they had something the sellers wanted in return. Trade was made simpler by the invention of coins in Lydia in the 7th century BC. The Greeks copied Lydian coins. This gave traders portable pieces of metal with a guaranteed value. Merchant ships carrying coins were even more attractive to pirates.

THE KYRENIAN SHIP

DISCOVERY
In 1967, a well-preserved merchant ship was found by the Greek diver Andreas Kariolou, near Kyrenia in Cyprus. Many of the ship's timbers were intact, protected by layers of sand. The ship was 14.75 m (48 ft) long and 3.4 m (11 ft 2 in) wide, and made of pine planks held together by oak pegs. When it sank, the ship was 80 years old and had already been repaired many times.

LIFE AT SEA
Before the Kyrenian ship was found, we only had vase paintings like this to tell us about the Greeks' life at sea. Finds from the ship provided more information. Four sets of bowls and spoons indicated that there was a crew of four men. Olive stones, fig seeds, and a garlic clove show the foods the sailors ate. Lead fishing weights were found, suggesting that the crew fished as they travelled.

CARGO
About 9,000 almonds, still in their shells, were found in the shipwreck. Such a large number must have been part of the cargo rather than supplies for the voyage. There were also 404 *amphorae* (wine or oil jars) of several different types. Some of these came from Rhodes and some from Samos. This suggests the ship had been loaded with its goods at different ports.

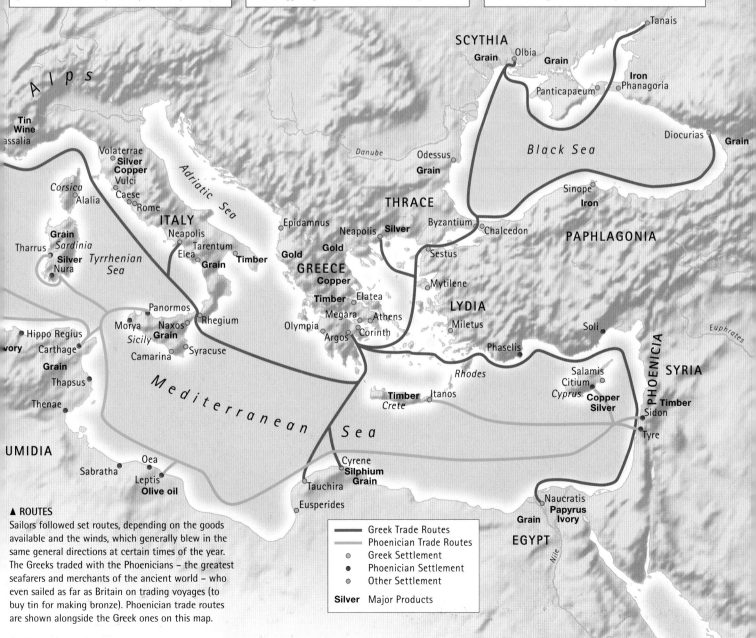

▲ ROUTES
Sailors followed set routes, depending on the goods available and the winds, which generally blew in the same general directions at certain times of the year. The Greeks traded with the Phoenicians – the greatest seafarers and merchants of the ancient world – who even sailed as far as Britain on trading voyages (to buy tin for making bronze). Phoenician trade routes are shown alongside the Greek ones on this map.

Legend:
— Greek Trade Routes
— Phoenician Trade Routes
○ Greek Settlement
● Phoenician Settlement
○ Other Settlement
Silver Major Products

GODS

The Greeks worshipped many different gods, each of which, they believed, ruled over a different area of their lives. The most important gods belonged to one family led by Zeus, the king of the gods. Greek writings show that people had different attitudes to their gods. While most people believed in the powers of the gods and feared angering them, others doubted that they even existed.

Athena Polias mourns Athenians killed in war

◄ FATHER OF GODS
Zeus was responsible for weather – bringing rain and storms. In art, he was often shown armed with a thunderbolt. He was also the god of justice and protector of strangers. Zeus was the father of many other gods, including Athena, the goddess of wisdom. This bronze statue, believed to show Zeus, was found in a shipwreck off the coast of Athens.

▲ ROLES OF THE GODS
Each god had different roles and often different names to go with each role. For example, Athena Polias ("of the *polis*") was the special protector of the *polis* – Athens in particular. As Athena Promachos ("she who fights in front") she was the goddess of war, fighting in the front line of Greek armies. As Athena Ergane ("the worker") she watched over craftsmen, such as potters.

gods

▲ APOLLO AND ARTEMIS
Apollo and his twin sister Artemis were both archer gods associated with sickness – sending sudden death with their arrows – and healing. Artemis was the goddess of childbirth, hunting, and the moon, while Apollo was the god of prophecy, poetry, and music. He was also a god of light, known as Phoebus ("shining"). In art, he was always shown as a perfect *ephebe* – a beardless youth.

◄ MOUNT OLYMPUS

The highest mountain in the Greek mainland is Olympus which was believed to be the home of the Olympians – the 12 most important gods. These were Aphrodite, Apollo, Ares, Artemis, Athena, Demeter, Dionysus, Hephaestus, Hera, Hermes, Poseidon, and Zeus. Olympus originally existed only in myth. Later, the same name was given to this actual peak.

HADES AND PERSEPHONE ►

Hades, the brother of Zeus, was the god who ruled the underworld – land of the dead. According to myth, he kidnapped Demeter's daughter Persephone and carried her off to the underworld. Demeter was so unhappy about this that she refused to let crops grow, causing winter. Zeus then allowed Persephone to return for part of the year, bringing spring and summer with her.

Hades

Persephone

OTHER GODS

ARES

Ares, the god of war, was thought to enjoy violence and destruction, not caring which side he fought on. He was known as Alloprosallos, meaning "leaning first to one side and then the other". Ares was an untrustworthy god, who was feared rather than worshipped. The Spartans had a shrine to Ares where his statue was chained, to stop him running away to fight on the side of Sparta's enemies.

APHRODITE

Aphrodite, the beautiful goddess of love, was supposedly born in the sea, then rode to shore on a scallop shell. She first stepped on land on the island of Cyprus. Aphrodite was powerful enough to make gods and mortals fall in love against their wishes. She caused the Trojan War, by making Helen, wife of King Menelaus of Sparta, fall in love with the Trojan prince Paris.

HERMES

Hermes was the messenger of the gods. He was also in charge of roads and boundaries, merchants, and thieves. Stone "herms" (rectangular columns topped with the god's head) stood as guardian figures on street corners and in gateways in Athens. In art, he was shown with winged shoes and the staff of a herald, or messenger. He invented the lyre, the alphabet, and boxing.

POSEIDON

Zeus's other brother Poseidon was the god of the sea, usually shown with a trident (fishing spear). He was worshipped by sailors who called him Poseidon Pontios ("of the sea") and Porthmios ("granter of safe passages"). As Poseidon Enosichthon ("earthshaker") he was thought to cause earthquakes whilst angry. Poseidon was said to keep a gold chariot and white horses in an underwater palace.

RELIGIOUS CEREMONIES

Religious ceremonies usually took place in the open air, inside a *temenos* ("sanctuary"), a special sacred place away from ordinary day-to-day activities. The *temenos* contained an altar and sometimes a temple, looked after by priests and priestesses. For the Greeks, religion played a major part in everyday life, and everyone took part in prayers and religious ceremonies for the gods.

▲ ALTAR

The altar was where people communicated with gods, offering prayers and sacrifices. Altars came in many shapes and sizes, from small plain stone blocks to this vast, elaborately decorated altar to Zeus at Pergamum. Those in danger, such as runaway slaves, threw themselves on the mercy of the gods at the altar. Killing anyone here would bring the god's anger on the whole *polis*.

▲ FESTIVALS

Every *polis* had its own calendar of festivals, which included sacrifices and processions, as well as sporting and theatrical competitions. It was believed that the gods enjoyed these events as much as the people. A hymn to Apollo describes his festival on Delos: "There with their long robes trailing, Ionians gather together, treading your sacred road, with their wives and children about them. There they give you pleasure with boxing and dancing and singing, calling aloud on your name." In this painting of a festival, a winged goddess helps to lead the ox to the sacrifice, while men with torches dance around her.

SACRIFICES ▶

This statue shows a man carrying a calf to an altar to be sacrificed. Sheep, goats, pigs, and cattle were killed as sacrificial offerings. The choice of animal usually depended on what the worshipper could afford. Fruit or cakes were also "sacrificed" by leaving them on an altar. A third type of sacrifice was the "libation" of liquid – milk, wine, olive oil, or blood – which was poured onto the ground.

religious ceremonies

SACRIFICIAL RITUALS

PROCESSION
The first stage in a sacrifice was to lead the animal, often wearing a floral garland, in a procession to the altar. Pipe playing and the singing of hymns usually accompanied the procession. The worshippers took turns to throw barley on the altar fire. This allowed them all to share in the act of sacrifice and win the goodwill of the god.

PRAYER
The person making a sacrifice at the altar (often a priest) said a prayer. This called on the god and asked for a specific favour, such as victory in war, good health, or a successful harvest. While he prayed, the worshipper would hold out his hands with the palms upwards for the gods who lived on Mount Olympus, and downwards for gods of the underworld.

KILLING
The animal's head was held back and its throat was cut with a knife. Large animals, such as oxen, were often stunned first with a hammer. At the moment of death, the women raised a cry, and blood was poured over the altar. This was collected in bowls from large animals. Small animals, such as this pig, were held over the altar.

LIVER
The next stage in the sacrifice was to cut the animal's belly open to examine its inner organs, especially the liver. The state of the liver indicated whether the god was pleased with the sacrifice. An odd-shaped or diseased liver meant that the sacrifice had been rejected, and a new animal would then have to be offered in its place.

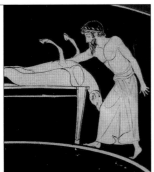

FEAST FOR THE GOD
After the animal had been butchered, a portion of it was reserved for the god, usually the thigh bones, which were wrapped in fat. These bones were tied to a long metal spit and burned on the altar. The Greeks believed the rising smoke carried the gift up to the god. At the same time, a libation of wine was poured over the altar.

Child

Folded robe

▲ ATHENA'S BIRTHDAY
The most important festival in Athens was the Panathenaia, held in late summer for Athena's birthday. Every four years, a bigger version of the festival, the Great Panathenaia, was also celebrated. The most important part of this was the gift of a new robe to the sacred wooden statue of the goddess. This relief from the Parthenon shows the folded robe being passed from a child to a priest.

▼ PURITY
The *temenos* ("sanctuary") was subject to strict rules of purity. People in contact with childbirth or death were regarded as polluted, or unclean, and in danger. They had to perform acts of purification (ritual cleansing) before they could enter the *temenos* again. A house where someone had given birth or died might be purified with sea water or the powerful smoke of burning sulphur.

Sulphur fumes

ORACLES AND DIVINATION

The Greeks believed that their gods took a close interest in human affairs, and gave advice and warnings in various ways. Natural events, such as earthquakes, the flight of birds, or even a sneeze (a lucky sign) were signs from the gods. There were also special holy places, such as Delphi and Dodona, where gods communicated through oracles. These might be given by rustling leaves, clanging pots, or human mediums in a trance. The word "oracle" referred both to the message given by the god and to the place where the god was consulted.

▲ DODONA
The oldest oracle of all, described by Homer, was that of Zeus at Dodona (in northwest Greece), where the god spoke through the rustling of leaves or by the sound and movement of doves in a sacred oak tree. In Homer's time, the oracles were interpreted by priests known as *selloi*, who slept beneath the tree and never washed their feet. A younger oak tree now grows where the ancient one stood.

◄ QUESTIONS FOR THE GOD
People at Dodona wrote down the question they wished to ask Zeus on lead tablets. Many have been found here and at the site of other oracles. They illustrate the sort of problems that made people travel far to consult a god. Questions asked include "Nicocrateia would like to know to what god she ought to sacrifice to in order to get well and feel better and make her illness go away?" and "Has Peistos stolen the wool from the mattress?".

LEAD TABLETS
FOUND AT
DODONA

oracles

◄ THE DELPHIC ORACLE
The oracle with the greatest prestige was that of Apollo at Delphi. This was consulted both by private individuals and also by official representatives of *poleis* who sought advice on important business, such as going to war, founding a colony, or considering any religious matter, such as the building of a new temple. Many gifts were given to the oracle by those seeking answers, and as a result Delphi grew very rich. This is evident in the impressive ruins still there today, such as this circular *tholos*, the purpose of which remains a mystery.

Pythia

◄ APOLLO'S PRIESTESS

At Delphi, Apollo's oracles were given by a priestess, known as the Pythia, who sat on an uncomfortable three-legged bronze bowl called a tripod. While shaking a branch of laurel, she entered into a trance as she was taken over by the god. This Athenian vase painting shows the Pythia answering a questioner with her head bowed – a sign of her trancelike state. The questioner carried a sacred cake from Apollo's temple as an offering for the god.

Tripod

OTHER ORACLES

FLAMES

There were many other oracles in Greece, where various methods were used to interpret the messages of the gods. At Olympia, there was an oracle of Zeus in which the behaviour of flames on an altar was studied carefully. Bright, strong flames were taken as a good sign from Zeus. This method is called pyromancy.

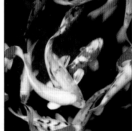

FISH

At Sura in what is now called Turkey, there was an oracle of Apollo, where the god was believed to communicate through the behaviour of sacred fish. The questioner tried to feed the fish. If the fish seized the food it was a good sign; but if they refused to eat, it was interpreted as a sign of disaster.

DICE

The hero Heracles had his own oracle at Bura in western Greece. People who wished to ask a question prayed in front of his statue, then threw dice. For each possible combination of numbers, there was a different interpretation, such as "You will be successful" or "You should go on a long journey".

Owl sacred to Athena

◄ DIVINERS

Signs from the gods were also interpreted by diviners. In one method, a diviner faced north to scan the sky for birds. A bird flying from the right (east) was seen as a lucky sign, while one flying from the left (west) was unlucky. Before the Battle of Salamis, when the Athenians defeated the Persians, diviners were overjoyed to see an owl fly from the right and land on an Athenian ship – especially lucky, because the owl was Athena's bird.

▲ SACRIFICIAL DIVINATION

Another form of divination, called hieromancy, involved examining the entrails of sacrificial animals – the liver, in particular. A smooth, healthy liver was lucky, but a diseased or unusual-looking liver was a bad sign and a warning sent by the gods. Although hieromancy took place at an altar, as in this wall painting of a sheep sacrifice, it could be performed anywhere and by anyone. Hieromancy was regarded as a science, and there were manuals explaining how it should be done.

DEATH AND THE AFTERLIFE

The Greeks had various ideas about what happened to them after death. Some thought that the "shades" of the dead (ghostlike forms of the living person) inhabited a miserable, dark underworld ruled by Hades. There was also a common belief that the dead could receive offerings in their tombs. Providing the dead with a proper funeral helped to ensure that they would not come back to haunt the living. Caring for the tomb was an important duty carried out by every family.

◄ SHADES
In the *Odyssey*, Odysseus visits the underworld and sees the shades of the dead, which Homer describes as wretched batlike creatures flitting about in cold, dark, echoing halls. He meets the shade of his old comrade, Achilles, and congratulates him on his fame, telling him, "Do not grieve at your death". Achilles replies, "I'd rather be a day-labourer on earth working for a poor man than lord of all the hosts of the dead."

Achilles as a youthful spirit

Odysseus

Sword used to sacrifice lamb

Slaughtered lamb

JOURNEY TO THE UNDERWORLD ▲
The souls of the dead were thought to be taken to the underworld by the god Hermes. He handed them over to the old boatman, Charon (shown above), who ferried them across the River Acheron to the kingdom of Hades. The dead had to pay Charon a small fee to cross the river, so a coin was placed in the mouth of the corpse during the funeral preparations. Hermes and Charon both appear on this container used for making offerings at funerals.

FUNERAL RITES

LAYING OUT
On the day of death, the corpse was laid out on a couch by the closest female relatives, who closed its mouth and eyes, and washed, perfumed, and dressed it, adorning it with flowers. For two days, mourners came to pay their last respects, including women dressed in black who sang laments and tore their hair.

◀ ORACLE OF THE DEAD

There was an oracle of the dead at Ephyra in northwest Greece, where people believed they could consult the spirits of the dead. Ephyra is beside the Acheron, a real river thought to flow into the underworld. The site includes a series of rooms and an underground chamber carved out of rock. People came to be reunited with lost loved ones, and to seek their advice.

GIFT FOR PERSEPHONE ▶

Visitors to Ephyra moved from dark room to dark room, before descending into the underground chamber, where they believed they were entering the underworld. To be protected from harm, they had to win the goodwill of Persephone, wife of Hades and queen of the dead. They left behind small pottery models of her as offerings.

Braided hair

Bronze vessel

e▸▸ death

Clytemnestra, queen of Mycenae, murders Cassandra (her husband's slave), in a scene from the myth of Agamemnon

◀ GHOSTS

People who had not received a proper funeral, or who had died unnatural deaths, could come back to haunt the living. Murder victims, believed to be particularly vengeful, sometimes had their hands cut off by those who buried them, and placed under their armpits to render them powerless. Those killed in battle could also return. The travel writer, Pausanias, claimed that on the battlefield at Marathon, "All night you can hear horses whinnying and men fighting."

FUNERAL PROCESSION
Before dawn on the third day after a death, the body was wrapped in a shroud and covered in a cloak. It was then carried by horse and cart to the graveyard, accompanied by a procession called the *ekphora*. In the Archaic Age, when this vase was painted, the wealthy used chariots for the procession.

BURIAL
The body might be cremated or buried, depending on family preferences or special circumstances. Children were rarely cremated. The body or urn of ashes was buried along with possessions, such as pottery, jewels, or other personal belongings. Children were often buried with their favourite toys.

MEMORIAL
Those who could afford it would set up a memorial on the site of a loved one's tomb. This took the form of a small monument or a carved stone slab called a *stele*. A typical *stele* might show a touching farewell scene with the dead man or woman offering a hand to the child, wife, or husband they had left behind.

OFFERINGS
The dead were given libations (liquid offerings) of water, oil, honey, and wine. These were poured from vases called *lekythoi*, which were also buried as offerings. This was done at the funeral, then nine days later, and once a year thereafter. This *lekythos* shows a woman bringing offerings to a tomb.

PURIFICATION
The Greeks believed that a dead body defiled everyone who came into contact with it, and so the mourners and house had to be purified. After the funeral, the mourners washed with spring water, which was placed in a vessel outside the house. The house was also purified with water and sprigs of hyssop.

CORINTHIAN
HELMETS

WARFARE

The Greeks' rivalry and extreme competitiveness led to almost constant fighting between *poleis*. As a result, warfare, both on land and at sea, was central to Greek life, and seen as a fairly normal state of affairs. Every Greek man believed it was his duty to kill his enemies and to help his friends. Fighting also provided men with the opportunity to win the praise and approval of their fellow citizens. Greeks killed in battle were honoured with public funerals and speeches praising their bravery.

THE PHALANX

These warriors are hoplites, named after the large *hoplon*, or shield, they carried Hoplites fought in a tight group called a phalanx - a wall of warriors with their shields locked together. Each hoplite raised his spear and thrust it down towards the enemy hoplites, jabbing at the exposed area between their shield and the helmet. This vase shows two phalanxes marching towards each other. The phalanx on the left is accompanied by a boy pipe player, whose music helped the hoplites to march in time.

▲ ARMOUR
Greek warriors wore greaves (shin guards), a breastplate or linen corslet, and a bronze helmet, which came in several styles. The most popular style was the Corinthian helmet. This covered the whole head except the eyes and mouth. Armour was worn for display as well as protection, and helmets were fitted with tall horsehair crests for decoration.

Sheet of bronze beaten into helmet shape

RAVAGING ▶
Although war was frequent, big battles were rare. Far more common was ravaging – invading enemy territory at harvest time to destroy crops and vines, and burn farm buildings. After Athens and Sparta went to war in 431 BC, the Spartan army regularly invaded Attica, the land of Athens, and destroyed the farmers' crops. The Spartans hoped to provoke the Athenians into fighting a battle to defend their farms. Fearing the Spartans' fighting reputation, however, the Athenians refused to be drawn into battle.

warfare

Liver

◄ ON THE MARCH
Many rituals surrounded Greek warfare, such as sacrificing animals before battle. This soldier is inspecting the liver of an animal, which was believed to carry omens, or messages from the gods. A smooth, healthy liver meant that it was a good day to fight a battle. While they marched, the soldiers sang *paeans* – hymns addressed to the gods to ward off evil. After battle, the victorious army made a trophy by hanging enemy armour from a tree as proof of their victory. This was offered as a gesture of thanksgiving to the gods.

Hoplite

RITUALS ►
The Spartans took the religious side of war more seriously than other Greeks. Marching Spartan soldiers carried a sacred flame from the altar of Zeus in Sparta, which was kept burning continually. They also took a flock of sheep with them to sacrifice. Spartans only fought after they received a good omen from a sacrifice. At the battle of Plataea, in 479 BC, they sat under a hail of Persian arrows, sacrificing sheep after sheep, until they received a good omen and started fighting back.

Sheep for sacrifice

TYPES OF SOLDIER

HOPLITES
Hoplites were the main attacking force in Greek armies. Unlike the rowers in the Athenian navy, who were poor, hoplites belonged to the wealthier classes of a *polis*. Their armour was expensive and of high quality, and they had to pay for it themselves. This hoplite is wearing an Attic helmet, which had no nose guard, and left the ears uncovered. This improved the hoplite's hearing but gave him less protection than a Corinthian helmet.

HORSEMEN
Cavalry played a minor role in the 5th century BC, working as scouts and pursuing fleeing enemies. The stirrup had not yet been invented, so riders were not securely mounted. During one military campaign, the Athenian general Xenophon told his hoplites: "We are on a much more solid footing than cavalrymen, who are up in the air on horseback and afraid not only of us but of falling off their horses." This bronze rider is wearing a Corinthian helmet.

PELTASTS
Before the hoplite phalanxes clashed in battle, archers, slingers (who fired stones), and peltasts, armed with javelins (throwing spears), fired on the enemy from a distance to pick off individual soldiers. Peltasts were named after their *pelte* – a crescent-shaped shield made of wickerwork covered with sheep or goatskin. A peltast rushed towards the hoplite phalanx, hurled his javelin, and then ran quickly away before the slower hoplites could catch him.

THE PERSIAN WARS

In the 5th century BC, the Greeks united to defend themselves against a single enemy. Between 550 and 510 BC, the Persians conquered a huge empire, stretching from Egypt to the edge of India. In 499 BC, the Ionian Greeks (living on what is now the Turkish coast) rebelled against Persian rule. They were helped by Athens. The Persian king, Darius, crushed the revolt, then determined to punish the Athenians, and conquer Greece.

▲ PHEIDIPPIDES
In 490 BC, the Persians landed at Marathon in Attica. An Athenian athlete, Pheidippides, ran to Sparta to ask for help, covering some 233 km (145 miles) in only two days (modern marathon running was inspired by this). The Spartans promised to come as soon as they had finished celebrating a religious festival.

◄ HIGH KING DARIUS
After crushing the Ionian revolt, Darius sent messengers to the mainland Greeks to demand "earth and water" – a traditional sign of submission. In Athens his messengers were thrown into a pit, while the Spartans dropped them down a well, telling them to fetch their own earth and water! Darius is shown here in a relief at Persepolis, his capital city.

Regal staff

Persian wars

GENERAL MILTIADES

MARATHON ▲
The Athenian general Miltiades was heavily outnumbered, but he decided to attack the Persians on the shore at Marathon. The result was an astonishing victory. The Persians lost 6,400 men while only 192 Athenians were killed. The Spartans reached Marathon too late for the battle, but praised the Athenians for their fighting skills.

XERXES ►

Ten years after the battle of Marathon, there was an even larger Persian invasion, led by Darius' son Xerxes. He used ships to build two bridges across the Hellespont (the narrow channel separating Asia and Europe), and for the next seven days and nights his vast army marched across. Many Greeks accepted Persian rule without a fight, but 31 *poleis*, led by Sparta, united in a league to fight the invaders.

Xerxes, sheltered from the sun by a parasol

LEONIDAS ►

At Thermopylae, the Spartan general Leonidas and his army put up a brave but hopeless fight. They fought so fiercely that the Persian soldiers had to be whipped towards them by their officers. When the Spartans' spears were broken, they drew their swords and fought until every last one of them was killed. Leonidas is still a great hero to the Greeks. Modern statues of the king stand at Thermopylae and Sparta.

▲ THERMOPYLAE

The Greek army planned to block off the Persians' route in a narrow pass at Thermopylae. When the Persians found a way around the pass, the Spartan king Leonidas ordered most of his army to retreat. He stayed behind with around 300 Spartans. Leonidas knew that his position was hopeless but said that he had decided "to die for Greece". In this artwork by Peter Connolly, the Spartan phalanx can be seen advancing towards the Persians, under a heavy shower of arrows.

THE PERSIAN EMPIRE (5TH CENTURY BC)

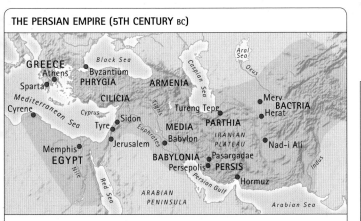

At the height of its power, the Persian Empire stretched from Egypt to the edge of India. It was divided into more than 20 provinces, each ruled on behalf of the king by a *satrap*, or governor. Each province was expected to pay financial tribute to the king, and any rebellion was ruthlessly crushed. However, Persian rule was usually not harsh, and the various different lands of the empire were permitted to keep their individual cultures, languages, and religions. As a result, most of the conquered peoples felt no need to revolt. The Greeks, with their love of political freedom, were the exception.

HERODOTUS

Almost everything we know about the Persian wars comes from the writings of Herodotus. Born in Halicarnassus in Ionia c.484 BC, Herodotus was the first real historian. He even gave us the word "history" in the title of his book, *Historia* (originally meaning "inquiry"). Although he was a Greek, Herodotus was a fair writer who showed both the Greek and Persian points of view. He travelled widely to research his histories, interviewing people and collecting their stories. In the first sentence of the book, he said his plan was "to put on record the astonishing achievements both of our own and of other peoples."

THE BATTLE OF SALAMIS

Following the Persian victory at Thermopylae in August 480 BC, the whole of Greece lay open to invasion. When the Persians first invaded, the Athenians had asked the Delphic oracle for advice. Th oracle warned that Athens was doomed but that "the wooden wall alone shall not fall, but save you and your children". Themistocles Athens' leading general, convinced his fellow citizens that "wooder wall" meant Athenian ships. He persuaded them to fight a sea battl In September 480 BC, the people crossed the sea to Troezon, Aegina and Salamis, where the fleet awaited the Persians.

◄ THEMISTOCLES

Themistocles fought as a young man at Marathon, and was convinced that the Persians would return one day. He persuaded his fellow Athenians to use funds from the state silver mines at Laureion to enlarge the navy from 70 to 200 ships. He also created a new fortified harbour for Athens at Piraeus. Previously, the Athenians used to beach their ships on the unprotected shore of Phalerum bay.

e▸▸
Battle of Salamis

SEA VICTORY ►
One Athenian eyewitness, the playwright Aeschylus, wrote of the Persians that "their dense numbers, confined in the narrow seas, had no room for action. They cracked their oars, and struck each other with their beaks of bronze". Meanwhile the Greek *triremes* repeatedly rammed the Persian ships. This picture shows a *trireme*, steered by the helmsman at the rear, smashing into the side of a Persian ship with the aim of breaking its oars and tipping it over.

▲ SALAMIS
The Greek fleet at Salamis numbered 380 ships, of which 180 were Athenian and the rest from other Greek *poleis*. They were outnumbered by the Persians, who had around 500 ships. Themistocles' plan was to fight a battle in the narrow waters between Salamis and the mainland, where the Persian fleet would be crowded together and therefore less effective.

XERXES AND THE BATTLE OF SALAMIS

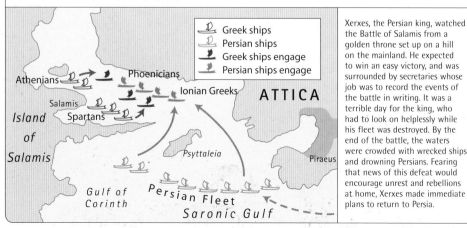

Key:
- 🚢 Greek ships
- 🚢 Persian ships
- 🚢 Greek ships engage
- 🚢 Persian ships engage

Athenians
Phoenicians
Salamis
Ionian Greeks
ATTICA
Island of Salamis
Spartans
Psyttaleia
Piraeus
Gulf of Corinth
Persian Fleet
Saronic Gulf

Xerxes, the Persian king, watched the Battle of Salamis from a golden throne set up on a hill on the mainland. He expected to win an easy victory, and was surrounded by secretaries whose job was to record the events of the battle in writing. It was a terrible day for the king, who had to look on helplessly while his fleet was destroyed. By the end of the battle, the waters were crowded with wrecked ships and drowning Persians. Fearing that news of this defeat would encourage unrest and rebellions at home, Xerxes made immediate plans to return to Persia.

◄ ATHENS SACKED
After the Athenians abandoned their city, it was captured and sacked by the Persians (before and after their defeat), who burned the sacred temples on the Acropolis. To every Greek, the destruction of these temples was an unforgiveable crime. The broken statues were later buried on the Acropolis, where they were discovered by archaeologists hundreds of years later.

DAMAGED STATUE FROM THE TEMPLE OF ATHENA

Greek hoplite

Persian soldier

DISGRACED HERO ►
Themistocles, the hero of Athens, ended his life in disgrace – he was accused of being arrogant and taking bribes. In about 470 BC, he was ostracized from Athens, and then accused of plotting with the Persians. He fled to Persia and threw himself on the mercy of Xerxes. The king welcomed his old enemy and is said to have called out repeatedly in his sleep for joy, "I have Themistocles the Athenian!"

Themistocles named for ostracism

▲ PERSIAN DEFEAT
After Salamis, Xerxes returned to Persia and left behind part of his army, led by his general, Mardonius. The Greeks then attacked. Led by the Spartan, Pausanias, they gathered a force of 38,700 men – the largest Greek army yet assembled. In 479 BC, the Greeks met Mardonius at Plataea in Boeotia and won a final victory. The Persian threat to Greece was over.

Helmsman

Space for 170 oarsmen

Soldiers on deck fought with spears and bows

THE ATHENIAN EMPIRE

In 478 BC, Athens became the leader of a league of seafaring *poleis* that waged war against Persia together. The aims of the league were to free any Greek peoples still under Persian control, to get revenge for Xerxes' acts of destruction by raiding his land, and to prevent any further Persian threat. Little by little, the Athenians increased their control over their allies, until they had transformed the league into their own empire.

Abdera
Strepsa
Argilus
Galepsus
Methone
Stolos
Thasos
Aenea
Potidaea
Singus
Hephaestia
Scione
Torone
Lemnos
Aegean Sea
GREECE
Peparethos
Skyros
Chalcis
Thebes
Styra
Andros
Corinth
Aegina
Athens
Argos
Mykonos
PELOPONNESE
Naxos
Sparta
Melos

LEAGUE TERRITORY ► This map shows the Athenian empire during the 470s BC. Some of the Greek *poleis* freed from Persian rule were forced to join the league. On Naxos, Andros, and elsewhere, Athens also founded new settlements, called *cleruchies*, whose settlers kept their Athenian citizenship. These served as overseas garrisons, extending Athenian control.

Ostrakon *shows the message "Cimon (son of) Miltiades"*

◄ CIMON From 479 to 463 BC, most of the league's campaigns were commanded by the Athenian general Cimon, son of Miltiades, the famous victor of Marathon. Under Cimon, the league won a series of victories over the Persians, driving them from the coasts of Ionia and Thrace. Despite his successes, Cimon had many enemies at home, including Pericles. In 461 BC, Cimon's enemies ostracized him from Athens.

◄ TREASURY In 454 BC, the treasury (monetary centre) of the league was moved from Delos to Athens, supposedly for safekeeping. In the same year, the Athenians began to display yearly records of financial contributions on stone tablets on the Acropolis. Each tablet lists the amount – one-sixtieth of the overall contribution from each *polis* – allocated to Athens itself as a tax. In effect, the league members were now paying tribute to the leading member of the league.

***Ionic columns** at Delos*

◄ LEAGUE OF DELOS The alliance against Persia was known as the Delian League, named after the sacred island of Delos, where the member states first met. Athens, as the greatest naval power, became the leader of the league, which the other *poleis* were happy to accept. Each member was required to provide ships or money for the league's fleet. The type of contribution was decided by Athens, which also supplied the naval commanders. The delegates who met at Delos threw lumps of iron into the sea and swore not to desert the alliance until the iron rose again to the surface – which they knew would never happen.

MODERN REPLIC
OF A TRIREME

Byzantium
Chalcedon

Sea of Marmara

psacus
Cyzicus

epsis

ene

Phocaea

ASIA
MINOR

Erythrae
Lebedus

s

Priene
Miletus

Idyma

os

Cnidus
Telmessus
Ialysus

Nisyros

Lindos

Rhodes

COIN DECREE

In about 440 BC, the Athenians issued a decree forbidding league members to make their own coins. They had to use Athenian coins, showing the goddess Athena's head. This had no economic benefit for Athens, but it was a way of demonstrating Athenian power, and undermining the freedom of the other *poleis*. In the event, the decree was never fully enforced.

PERICLES ►

From 440 BC, the leading Athenian general was Pericles. He had ambitious plans for the empire. In about 430 BC, he led a great naval expedition to the Black Sea to secure a safe supply of grain for Athens. He founded an Athenian base on the Hellespont – the strait between the Black Sea and the Aegean. Merchant ships sailing through the strait had to pay a tax to the Athenians there.

Corinthian helmet

◄ PEACE WITH PERSIA

By the middle of the 5th century BC, Persia was no longer a threat to the Greeks. In 449 BC, the Persian king, Artaxerxes (shown on this carved relief), made a peace agreement with the Athenians. There was no longer any reason why the league should continue, but the Athenians refused to disband it. When *poleis*, such as Samos, tried to leave the league, Athens forced them to rejoin. The Athenians punished rebellious *poleis* by increasing the contibutions they had to pay, and also by taking away their naval fleets.

Athenian empire

Oars

Furled sails

◄ GROWING POWERS

Most *poleis* found it simpler to pay money to Athens than to provide ships and crews. Between 454 and 431 BC, the number of states supplying ships fell from 17 to just two – Lesbos and Chios. The allies no longer built new ships or practised rowing them, so they lost their ability to fight at sea, whilst the Athenian navy grew in strength. Over time, the Athenians stopped referring to other league members as allies and instead described them as "the *poleis* which the Athenians rule".

THE PARTHENON

In the middle of the 5th century BC, Athens was at the height of its power. Yet the temples on the Acropolis, destroyed by the Persians in c.480 BC, still lay in ruins. Around 450 BC, Pericles persuaded the Athenian assembly to rebuild them. The building work was partly paid for with money from the allies. The Parthenon, a huge temple dedicated to the city's patron goddess Athena, was the centrepiece of the project. This monument to their victory over the Persians was a symbol of Athens that became famous around the world.

Parthenon

Pediment (once filled with statues)

▲ STATUE OF ATHENA
The sculptor Phidias (c.490–c.432 BC) created a huge statue of Athena from wood and precious materials. It measured 12 m (39 ft) in height. Her skin was made from hundreds of tiny strips of ivory from elephant tusks imported from Egypt, while her armour and clothing were made of 100 kg (220 lb) of gold. The original statue no longer exists, but some marble copies have survived.

MARBLE TEMPLE ▶
The Parthenon was built of sparkling white marble from Mount Pentelicon, 13 km (8 miles) northeast of Athens. Marble was such a prized building material that it was usually used only for sculptures. Building a whole temple from marble was a means of displaying Athens' wealth. The Parthenon, which even had marble roof tiles, required 22,000 tonnes (tons) of the stone.

Centaur (half-man, half-horse)

▲ METOPES
No Greek temple had more sculpted decoration than the Parthenon. Around the walls above the columns there were 92 relief panels, called *metopes*. These depicted scenes of combat drawn from myths – gods fighting giants, and Greek heroes fighting centaurs, Trojans, and female warriors called Amazons. These scenes reminded the Greeks of their struggle against the barbarians, and the Persian Wars. The painted backgrounds have mostly faded away, leaving only the sculptures, as seen here.

THE FRIEZE ▲

The most unusual feature of the Parthenon is a long frieze high up on the walls behind the columns, showing a religious procession in honour of Athena's birthday. It was previously unknown for humans to be depicted alongside gods and mythical heroes on a temple. The 192 male riders shown in the rieze may represent the dead heroes of the battle of Marathon.

THE PARTHENON

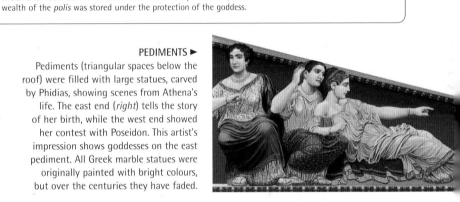

Marble roof

Acroterion (marble floral decoration)

Metope (red area)

Triglyph (blue area)

Frieze showing the Athenian procession

East pediment

This diagram shows the Parthenon as it would have looked when first built, with cutaways to reveal the interior. The *metopes*, with the mythical battle scenes, are around the outer walls, between blue-painted triglyphs. The frieze runs directly behind. The interior is divided into two rooms. The big room at the front, called the *cella*, housed Phidias' great statue of Athena. The smaller room behind it was used as the treasury of Athens, where the wealth of the *polis* was stored under the protection of the goddess.

Triglyph (panel carved with three ridges)

PEDIMENTS ▶

Pediments (triangular spaces below the roof) were filled with large statues, carved by Phidias, showing scenes from Athena's life. The east end (*right*) tells the story of her birth, while the west end showed her contest with Poseidon. This artist's impression shows goddesses on the east pediment. All Greek marble statues were originally painted with bright colours, but over the centuries they have faded.

COLUMN TYPES

DORIC
Greek temple architecture followed one of two styles, known as orders. Each order had strict design rules. The Parthenon's columns were built in the style of the Doric order, first seen on the Greek mainland. The sturdy columns had plain capitals (tops). The column itself was carved with 20 vertical grooves, called flutes, with sharp edges.

IONIC
The Ionic order, developed in Ionia, was chosen for the design of columns in the smaller temples on the Acropolis. Ionic columns are more delicate, with deeper flutes separated by raised flat ridges. Each Ionic column has two scrolls decorating its capital, and stands on a base. Doric columns do not have a base.

ATHENS AGAINST SPARTA

In 431 BC, a major war broke out between Athens and Sparta, which was head of a league of *poleis* on the mainland, mostly in the Peloponnese. The cause of the Peloponnesian War, as it was called, was Sparta's fear of the huge growth of Athens' power. Athens and her allies fought the Peloponnesian League for 27 years. The strength of Sparta was on land while Athens was a sea power, so it was a difficult war for either side to win.

FUNERAL SPEECH ▶

To keep up people's spirits, Pericles (495–429 BC) made a speech at the public funeral of the soldiers killed in the first year of the war. The speech praised the Athenian Empire: "Mighty indeed are the marks and monuments of our empire which we have left. Futures ages will wonder at us, as the present age wonders at us now."

THUCYDIDES

▲ THUCYDIDES

Thucydides, an Athenian general who fought in the war, wrote a long history of the conflict. He started writing at the outbreak of the fighting, convinced that it would be an important war worth remembering. He claimed that his work was "not a piece of writing designed to meet the needs of an immediate public, but was done to last for ever". His history is still read today and is our main source of information about the war.

Greek man remembered on a tombstone

▲ PLAGUE IN ATHENS

While the Spartans made annual summer invasions of Attica, burning the farmers' crops, the Athenians from the countryside took refuge behind the walls of the city. The overcrowded conditions led to a terrible plague, which broke out in 430 BC. Pericles was one of its victims.

Athenian hoplites

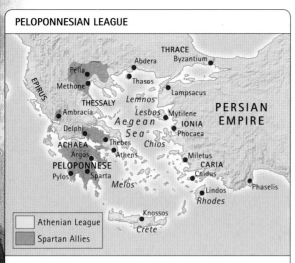

PELOPONNESIAN LEAGUE

THRACE
Abdera · Byzantium
Pella
Methone · Thasos
Lampsacus
Lemnos
THESSALY
Lesbos · Mytilene
Ambracia · Aegean · IONIA
Delphi · Sea · Phocaea
ACHAEA · Thebes · Chios
Argos · Athens · Miletus
PELOPONNESE · CARIA
Pylos · Sparta · Cnidus
Melos · Phaselis
Lindos
Rhodes
Knossos
Crete

PERSIAN EMPIRE
EPIRUS

- [ ] Athenian League
- [ ] Spartan Allies

Sparta was the head of a league of *poleis*, created as an alliance for mutual defense in the late 6th century BC. These *poleis* followed Sparta's lead in war and were expected to offer military assistance. Unlike the Athenian Empire, the league had no finances, and members remained independent. They did not pay financial tribute to Sparta. After Sparta, the most powerful *poleis* were Corinth, which provided a fleet of war ships, and Thebes. The war, fought between the Peloponnesian League and the Athenian Empire, also affected many other parts of the Greek world, and almost every *polis* took one side or the other.

Peloponnesian War

Hoplon (shield)

Chained prisoners

SPARTAN SURRENDER ▶
Sparta suffered a major setback in 425 BC when 420 Spartan hoplites were trapped by an Athenian fleet on the tiny waterless island of Sphacteria (near Pylos). After coming under a prolonged attack by archers and peltasts, the 292 surviving Spartans surrendered and were taken to Athens as prisoners. This was a great blow to their reputation since Spartan soldiers had always believed it was better to die than surrender.

▲ ALCIBIADES
In 415 BC, the politician Alcibiades convinced the Athenians to start a new war – against Syracuse in Sicily. He was about to lead the fleet, but was recalled to Athens, accused of crimes against religion. He fled to Sparta and offered to show the Spartans how to win the war. In Sicily, an entire Athenian army and fleet were destroyed.

▲ CHANGES IN FORTUNE
In 413 BC, Alcibiades persuaded the Spartans to build a fort in Attica as a refuge for runaway slaves from the Athenian silver mines. With less silver, Athens grew poorer while Sparta found new wealth from Persia. Hoping to recover the lost territories in Ionia, the Persians paid the Spartans to build a fleet to fight the Athenians at sea.

▲ SPARTAN VICTORY
In 405 BC, the Spartan general, Lysander, caught the Athenian fleet off guard at Aegospotami, and destroyed it. His own fleet cut off Athens' grain supply, and Athens was forced to surrender in 404 BC. The city walls, linking Athens with the port, were pulled down and the democratic system overthrown. Athens was never as powerful again.

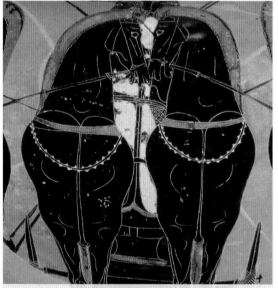

◄ TOMB PAINTINGS
The few surviving Greek paintings, such as this four-horse chariot from a tomb in Thrace, are found on the walls of tombs. Works painted by artists on wooden panels were of finer quality. *Stoas* and other public buildings, such as the gateway to the Athenian acropolis, served as art galleries, where famous paintings on panels were displayed for several centuries.

GREEK ART

Ancient Greece produced some of the most beautiful works of art the world has ever seen. Artists expressed themselves through many different forms, just as they do today. A large number of painted vases and marble statues have survived, but almost all Greek paintings have perished. Sculptors also worked with wood, gold and ivory, and bronze.

PERSEPHONE AND HADES ▲
This painting of Hades (god of the underworld) kidnapping Persephone comes from a Macedonian royal tomb. It is in a completely different style from the chariot painting, and was created by a very skilled artist. Full of energy, it has flowing lines and a rich use of colour, which gives us a sense of what the best Greek painting must have been like.

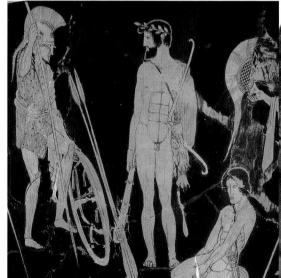

▲ "BLACK FIGURE" VASE
Greek vase painters had four colours to work with. The main two were red from fired clay, and black that was made of slip (liquid clay) containing iron oxide. Two other types of slip produced white and a darker red – both used for details. "Black figure" vases had figures, such as these horses, painted black. Lines for muscles were carved on the surface.

▲ "RED FIGURE" VASE
Around 530 BC, Athenian artists invented the "red figure" style, in which the background was painted black and the figures were left in the red of the clay. Details were painted on with a brush. This allowed for a freer and more flowing line than carving. Red was popular as it was closer in shade than black to the skin colour of Greek men and women.

Eyes of bone and glass

Teeth made of silver

◄ BRONZE WARRIOR

Bronze was so useful to the Greeks that almost all large bronze statues were melted down and reused. This statue survived because it was on a ship that sunk off the coast of Italy (where it was found in 1972). It was made using the "lost wax" method. A rough clay model was coated in a layer of wax, on which the finer details were carved. This was covered in clay to make a mould and then heated. The wax melted and flowed out of the mould, leaving a space which was filled with molten bronze.

▲ WONDER OF THE WORLD

Sculptors cast bronze in sections to make huge statues, called *colossi*. The most famous was the Colossus of Rhodes, a 34-m (111-ft) statue of the sun god, Helios, made by Chares of Lindos between 304 and 292 BC. It stood for 56 years before toppling in an earthquake. Even lying on the ground, it was seen as one of the Seven Wonders of the ancient world. The real statue stood on a hill, but it is often mistakenly shown bestriding the harbour.

► IVORY AND GOLD

The most costly statues were *chryselephantine*, which used strips of white elephant ivory (imported from Egypt) to create the appearance of skin, and gold for the hair and clothing. Very few *chryselephantine* statues have survived. This modern copy of the statue of Athena from the Parthenon gives us an idea of their amazing appearance.

Goatskin bearing the head of the snake-haired Medusa

THE OLYMPICS

While every *polis* had its own special festivals, there were also four great all-Greek sporting festivals. The most important was the festival of Zeus, held every four years at Olympia in southern Greece and open to all freeborn Greek males. Thousands of men and boys from all over the Greek world gathered here in a temporary encampment to take part and to watch. To allow Greeks to travel safely to Olympia, all wars were put on hold until the games were over.

▲ ZEUS'S HONOUR
The games, first held in 776 BC, were part of a religious festival in honour of Zeus, the king of the gods. His temple at Olympia held a gold-covered statue of him. It was 13 m (43 ft) high. This was one of the Seven Wonders of the ancient world. Outside the temple stood an altar – 30 m (98 ft) in circumference – made of ash left from thousands of sacrifices made to Zeus.

INTO THE STADIUM ▲
The stadium was 193 m (633 ft) long. Up to 45,000 Greek men and boys would watch each race. On the south side, there was a platform for judges and officials. This is the entrance to the stadium, or running track, at Olympia. The whole length was originally roofed over – athletes would walk down a dark tunnel before emerging into bright sunlight.

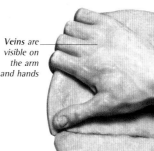

Veins are visible on the arm and hands

Split across discus has been repaired

Stadium (running track)

Temple of Zeus

DISCUS THROWER ▶
This marble statue of a discus thrower is a Roman copy of a lost bronze work, made in about 450 BC by an Athenian sculptor called Myron. It shows us how the discus was thrown. The athlete has brought his arm back behind him ready to swing it forward to release the discus. This is one of the most famous statues of an athlete ever made. Marble and bronze copies of it were common in Greek and Roman times.

◀ MEETING PLACE
The Olympic festival was much more than a sporting and religious event. The games provided a common dating system and helped develop a shared identity between different *poleis*. Olympia was also a place for exchanging ideas. Writers would read their latest works to large crowds, ambassadors came to negotiate treaties, artists to seek commissions, and merchants to trade.

Leonidaion (guest-house for important visitors)

olympics

◄ DEADLY GAME

The *pankration* (meaning "all force") was a combat sport – a mixture of boxing and wrestling – in which everything was allowed except biting and gouging. One contestant, Arrachion, was strangled while breaking his opponent's toe. At the moment of Arrachion's death, his opponent gave in from the pain in his foot. Arrachion was then declared the winner, and his dead body was crowned with an olive wreath.

THE EVENTS

THE FESTIVAL BEGINS

The festival began with a religious procession, then ceremonial oath-swearing by athletes and officials in front of Zeus' statue. Athletes swore they had trained properly and would compete fairly, while the judges swore that they would not be biased. Here, two athletes are seen washing as part of their preparation for the events.

DAY TWO

The second day of the games was devoted to chariot racing (for teams of two or four horses), horse racing, and the pentathlon. In this event, athletes (or pentathletes) threw the discus and javelin, wrestled, ran races, and competed at the long jump. It was a demanding competition to find the greatest all-round athlete.

DAY THREE

On the third day, there was a sacrifice of a hundred oxen, the thighs of which were burned on the great mound of ashes in front of the temple of Zeus. There would be boys' contests in running, wrestling, and boxing. For religious reasons, the third day of the games always took place when the moon was full.

DAY FOUR

Day four was taken up with men's foot races, wrestling, boxing, a race in armour, and the *pankration*. This bronze statue is of a boxer, whose face is battered by his many fights in sporting festivals. Instead of the gloves used today, leather thongs were tightly bound around a boxer's hands and wrists.

THE FINAL DAY

The Olympics ended with a prize-giving. The prizes, awarded by judges from Elis (the *polis* in charge of Olympia), were wreaths of wild olives. There was also a victors' banquet of meat from oxen sacrificed on the third day.

BRONZE DISCUS ►

Archaeologists have discovered some of the original equipment used by athletes in the games. This bronze discus, dating from the 6th century BC, was thrown by an athlete called Exoidas. He was so proud of his victory that he dedicated the discus to Castor and Pollux, twin sons of Zeus, and left it in their temple.

Exoidas' carved dedication

◄ CHARIOT RACING

The most exciting event was the chariot race. It was fast and dangerous, as up to 40 chariots, each pulled by four horses, hurtled round the track. The owners of the horses and chariots also received the glory of victory. The rich Athenian, Alcibiades, boasted, "I entered seven chariots for the chariot race, a larger number than any private individual before, took first, second and fourth place, and did everything in a grand style."

VICTORY OR DISGRACE ►

Victors had statues of themselves put up at Olympia and in their home cities, such as this statue of a victorious charioteer. Winning was all that mattered. The poet Pindar described the homecoming of unsuccessful wrestlers: "When they meet their mothers, they have no sweet laughter around them. In back streets out of their enemies' way they cower; disaster has bitten them."

THE THEATRE

MODEL OF A KING'S MASK FROM A TRAGEDY

Many of the words we use to do with theatre, including "drama", "actor", "scene", "comedy", and "tragedy", are Greek in origin. The reason is that theatre itself was invented by the Ancient Greeks, in Athens, some 2,500 years ago. Like the Olympic Games, theatrical performances were held as a competition, in which the prize of an ivy wreath went to the winning playwright. The plays were also part of a religious festival, held every spring in honour of Dionysus, god of drama, wine, and wild behaviour. In a play by Euripides, the god's worshippers declare, "Sing for joy! Praise Dionysus, god of joy!"

▲ ACTORS
Actors were always male. They wore masks allowing them to play many parts – male and female, old and young. It took a great deal of skill to do this, and actors spent years learning to use their bodies and voices to play a wide range of roles. This terracotta model shows an actor in a comedy.

MASKS ▲
Theatre masks had exaggerated features, which helped the audience members sitting in the upper rows to understand the emotions of the characters. Masks probably also acted as sound boxes, amplifying the voice and allowing actors to create powerful sound effects. Greek plays are full of wails and moans.

theatre

A GREEK THEATRE ▶
Greek theatres were always open-air, and usually built on hillsides. The name *theatron* ("viewing place") refers to the rows of seating rising up the hillside. Actors performed on a raised stage behind the circular *orchestra*, or dancing floor. This restored theatre at Epidaurus in the Peloponnese was one of the largest in Greece, and seats 14,000 people. It was so well-designed that even those in the highest row could hear every word spoken by the actors.

Seating, rising in circular tiers

▲ TRAGEDIES
The festival began with three days devoted to tragedies – plays showing the sufferings of heroes and heroines from myths. This vase painting shows the tragic heroine Electra, daughter of Agamemnon, who featured in plays by Aeschylus, Sophocles, and Euripides.

▲ SATYR PLAYS
At the end of each day of tragedies, there was light relief with a satyr play, also written by a tragic playwright. This was named after the chorus of satyrs – foolish, pleasure-seeking creatures with horses' tails. A satyr play was usually a light-hearted treatment of a mythical subject.

▲ COMEDY
The last day of the Athenian festival was devoted to comedy, when five playwrights each put on a single play. The most famous comic playwright was Aristophanes. His plays poked fun at leading Athenians, who would have been sitting in the audience, pretending not to mind.

◄ SPECIAL EFFECTS
Plays were full of special effects. The *mechane* ("flying machine"), or crane, was used to lower gods and heroes from the skies. The *ekkyklema* was a trolley that could be wheeled onto the stage. This vase shows the effects used in Euripides' play *Medea*. Medea has just murdered her own children, whose bodies are rolled out on the *ekkyklema*. As they are discovered, Medea appears above, using the flying machine, in a chariot pulled by serpents.

Medea's murdered children

CHORUS IN A MODERN-DAY PRODUCTION OF ONE OF SOPHOCLES' PLAYS

TRAGIC PLAYWRIGHTS

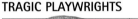

AESCHYLUS
Aeschylus wrote between 70 and 90 plays, winning first prize for the best tragic playwright at the festival some 13 times. He used a grand and formal style. Aeschylus believed that the gods acted justly, and his plays suggested the cause of suffering was evil or foolish human actions. He also fought at the battle of Marathon.

SOPHOCLES
The most sucessful tragedian was Sophocles, a general in the Athenian army who wrote 120 plays and won at least 20 first prizes. His style is more down-to-earth than that of Aeschylus. A typical plot features a scene in which the main character suddenly realizes that he or she has had a mistaken view of reality.

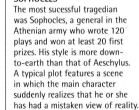

EURIPIDES
Euripides wanted to show how real people, especially women, would feel and behave in the strange circumstances of a myth. In total, he wrote 92 plays – some of them in a cave at Salamis – yet only won the prize for best play four times. After his death, he was seen as one of the greatest Greek writers.

◄ THE CHORUS
Actors were accompanied by a chorus – a group of men who sang songs, danced, and spoke as a group in the *orchestra*. Their role in a play was to question the actors, comment on the action, and explain the story to the audience. Unlike the actors, who were professionals, the chorus was made up of ordinary citizens who were not paid for taking part.

GREEK SCIENCE

The Greeks were the pioneers of science. Although earlier peoples charted the movement of the stars and made mathematical discoveries, they did not create general scientific principles or rules. The Greeks believed that the world could be understood using human reason. They also tested their ideas with experiments and used their discoveries to make inventions. Many sciences are still known by their Greek names, including geometry, astronomy, physics, biology, and mathematics.

science

◄ PYTHAGORAS

Pythagoras of Samos, who lived in the 6th century BC, was one of the founders of mathematics. He studied the patterns made by numbers, which he drew as dots forming shapes. For example, he drew the number four as four dots arranged in a square. Numbers that can be arranged to make squares, including 9, 16, and 25, are still called "square numbers". Pythagoras used such patterns to make discoveries, such as how to create different geometrical shapes, and measure their areas, angles, and the lengths of their sides. He believed that the universe was mathematical and tried to discover its secrets through numbers.

EUCLID

Euclid's
The Elements

EUCLID ►

The best-known Greek mathematician was Euclid. Little is known of his life except that he probably lived in Alexandria around 300 BC. His book *Stoicheia* (*The Elements*) summarizes the work of many earlier Greek mathematicians. Its principles have been used by mathematicians for more than 2,000 years and studied by generations of children. Euclid also wrote about optics – the science of light and vision. Ptolemy, king of Egypt, asked him if there was no quicker way to learn geometry than by studying his book. Euclid replied that "there is no royal road to geometry". This painting shows him using compasses to draw a circle.

MEASURING THE EARTH

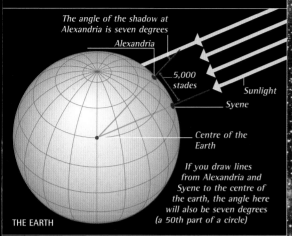

The angle of the shadow at Alexandria is seven degrees

Alexandria

5,000 stades

Sunlight

Syene

Centre of the Earth

If you draw lines from Alexandria and Syene to the centre of the earth, the angle here will also be seven degrees (a 50th part of a circle)

THE EARTH

Not only did Greek scientists know that the earth was round, one man also measured how big it was. Eratosthenes of Cyrene knew beforehand that at noon on midsummer day, the sun would be directly above Syene in Egypt, where its rays shone down a well. He then measured the angle of the sun's rays at the same time at Alexandria. Eratosthenes used the angle, which was seven degrees, to work out that the distance between the two places was roughly one-fiftieth of the circumference of the world. Since he knew the distance between Syene and Alexandria, he multiplied it by 50 to work out the size of the earth.

A SPHERICAL GLOBE ►
The philosopher and scientist Aristotle travelled widely and observed how different stars appeared in the sky, depending on how far north or south he was. Aristotle worked out "not only that the earth is spherical in shape, but also that it is a sphere of no great size: for otherwise the effect of so great a change of place would not be so quickly apparent."

ARCHIMEDES

INVENTIONS
The Sicilian Archimedes (287-211 BC) was an astronomer, mathematician, and brilliant inventor of war machines. During the Roman siege of Syracuse, he constructed huge mirrors, which directed sunlight on the enemy ships to set them on fire. He also invented giant claws, which used leverage to lift ships out of the sea.

MEASURING SPACE
Archimedes was asked by the tyrant of Syracuse to find if a crown he had made was pure gold or contained silver, a lighter metal. He worked out how to do this whilst in the bath, noticing that the water level rose when he got in. Archimedes realized that water could measure the amount of space taken up by an object.

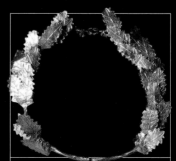

EUREKA!
Archimedes was so excited that he ran naked into the street shouting "Eureka!" ("I have found it"). Using his discovery, Archimedes measured the volume of a piece of pure gold of the same weight as the crown, both of which he placed in water. The crown displaced more water – it contained silver, which increased its volume.

DEATH
Archimedes was totally obsessed with mathematics. When the Romans captured Syracuse, he ignored warnings to flee, and continued to draw geometrical shapes in the sand. A Roman soldier ordered him to get up, but he refused to leave before solving the problem. The furious soldier killed him with his sword.

Tholos, where sacred snakes may have been kept

MEDICINE

Most Greeks believed that illnesses had supernatural causes, and could be treated only with the help of gods and, in particular, Asclepius, the god of healing. There were important shrines to Asclepius in many places, including Sicyon (west of Corinth), Athens, and Lebena on Crete. Sick people would go to these shrines and be treated by Asclepius' priests. Alongside this attitude, in the 5th century BC, a new scientific approach to medicine was developed by Hippocrates, who set up a school of medicine on the island of Cos.

▲ ASCLEPIUS

Like Heracles, Asclepius was a human who became a god after his death. He was said to be the son of another healing god, Apollo. According to a myth, Asclepius was so skilled at healing that he could bring the dead back to life. This angered Zeus who killed him with a thunderbolt.

medicine

▲ EPIDAURUS

The most famous of Asclepius' healing shrines, known as Asclepions, was at his birthplace, Epidaurus. This included a temple, hospital, and dwellings for priest-physicians. In many ways it resembled a modern health farm, set in beautiful surroundings with baths and a gymnasium. Here, practical treatments, medicines, changes of diet, exercise, and surgery were offered. Surgical tools, including scalpels and bone drills, have been found in Epidaurus.

Asclepius visits the patient in her dream

Asclepius uses his hands to heal

DREAM CURE ▶

The most important building at Epidaurus was the *abaton* (hall) where patients slept on a couch. They hoped to be visited in a dream by the god, who might treat them, or prescribe a treatment. Successful cures were recorded on tablets to display to visitors. One tells how Heraieus of Mytilene was cured of baldness: "Being ashamed because he was laughed at by others, he slept in the shrine. And the god, anointing his head with a drug, made him grow hair." Another man who had been unable to move was also cured. The god told him to heave the biggest boulder he could find into the sea!

Priests watch over a sleeping patient

VISITING THE DOCTOR

BLOOD LETTING
This vase painting from the 5th century BC shows a doctor treating a patient by letting blood, a common treatment used by Hippocrates' followers. It was done to restore the body's balance, reduce inflammation, slow a fast pulse, and help with pain. Influenced by Hippocrates, doctors bled patients until the 19th century.

SNAKE CURE
A snake climbing a tree can be seen at the top left of this relief depicting a sacrifice to Asclepius (sitting on the right). Snakes were sacred to the god, and a snake from Epidaurus would always be sent to a new Asclepion. The snakes were used in the healing rites, although exactly how they were used, no one knows.

DIET
This doctor is treating a boy. His belly is swollen and his ribs stick out. These are symptoms of malnutrition and were described in detail in medical texts by Hippocrates or his followers. Realizing the importance of food to the body, doctors placed great value on prescribing the correct diet for their patients.

HIPPOCRATIC OATH ▶
Hippocrates (c.469–399 BC), a doctor, teacher, and writer who lived on the island of Cos, has been called the "father of medicine". He helped to create a code for the way doctors should behave, which became known as the Hippocratic Oath. A student of medicine had to swear: "I will use my power to help the sick to the best of my ability and judgement; I will not harm or wrong any man by it." Today medical students still swear a version of a Hippocratic Oath when graduating from medical school.

MARBLE BUST OF
HIPPOCRATES

Marble votive probably referring to a cure for deafness

Papyrus with Hippocratic Oath written on it

▲ VOTIVES
Grateful patients left behind votives – small models made of pottery, metal, or carved from stone, showing the part of the body healed by the god. The selling of votives was a major source of income for the local people, and many votives have been found at Asclepions. This custom continues in Greek churches today, where votives are left for saints believed to have healing powers.

HIPPOCRATIC TEXTS ▲
Hippocrates believed that all diseases had natural causes, and so based his treatments on detailed observation of patients' symptoms. He aimed to do away with the superstitions surrounding sickness, such as the belief that they were caused by gods or evil spirits. Hippocrates' reputation was so great that his name was attached to many medical writings, called Hippocratic Texts, even though we do not know which of these, if any, he actually wrote.

PHILOSOPHY

The Greeks searched for answers to the big questions of existence. They invented philosophy (meaning "love of wisdom") – the study of the universe and the meaning of human behaviour. The first philosophers lived in Ionia in the 6th century BC, and discussed the cosmos and how it came into being. It was only after Socrates had asked "What is the right way to live?" – over a century later – that philosophers began to debate moral issues.

◄ SOCRATES

Socrates (c.469–399 BC) said that questions about the universe were pointless, and that what really mattered was human behaviour. He thought people only acted badly when they did not understand the difference between right and wrong. He never produced any written works, but his influence was so great that all philosophers who lived before him are called "pre-Socratic" ("before Socrates").

QUESTIONING BELIEFS ►

The poet Xenophanes of Colophon (c.580–480 BC) in Ionia criticized traditional Greek religious beliefs. He believed that people invented the gods and so imagined them to be human in form. He wrote that if horses could make images of gods, they would show them as horses.

PRE-SOCRATIC IDEAS

THALES
The very first recorded philosopher was Thales of Miletus, who was writing in about 580 BC. He was first to ask what materials made up the universe. Thales believed the answer was water. He wrote that everything was made of water, and the world floated on a vast water bed. The philosophers who followed Thales came up with many different answers to this question. None of Thales' writing survives today.

HERACLITUS
Writing in about 500 BC, Heraclitus of Ephesus argued that the basic substance of the universe was fire. He believed that everything is in a state of constant flux (movement), like a river, in which matter continually changes form. He said, "You cannot step into the same river twice." Other Greeks found his writing so hard to understand that he was nicknamed The Riddler and The Obscure.

PARMENIDES
In the 5th century BC, Parmenides of Elea in southern Italy wrote a poem in which he described the cosmos as a single object, shaped "like a well-rounded ball". He disagreed with Heraclitus, and claimed that nothing in the cosmos can ever change. He said that when things seemed to change, it was merely our senses fooling us. His ideas are even harder to understand than those of Heraclitus.

DEMOCRITUS
Democritus of Abdera lived in the late 5th century BC. He was nicknamed "the laughing philosopher", because he was so cheerful. He argued that the cosmos was endless, and was made up of tiny particles called atoms, moving around in space. An atom is a piece of matter so tiny that it cannot be split up into anything smaller. By their changes in position, atoms make up different types of matter.

Plato, holding his book Timaeus

Aristotle, holding his own book, Ethics

▲ PLATO

Plato (c.429-347 BC) was Socrates' greatest follower. Like Socrates, his main interest was humanity, but instead of looking at the behaviour of individuals, Plato also studied how people acted in societies. He founded the Academy – a school in the Athenian gymnasium – and lectured students on politics, law, and mathematics. In AD 1511, the Italian artist, Raphael, painted "The School of Athens", showing the leading Greek philosophers studying together.

ARISTOTLE ▶

Aristotle (384–322 BC) studied philosophy with Plato, but he had much wider interests than his teacher. He wrote books on subjects including philosophy, politics, geography, literature, art, biology, and natural history. He also invented the study of logic – the science of reasoning and argument. After tutoring Alexander the Great, he set up his own school in Athens at a gymnasium called the Lyceum.

Diogenes in his tub

◀ CYNIC

Diogenes of Sinope (c.400–325 BC) believed people should live in a natural state, concerned only with basic needs. He wore a shabby cloak, lived by begging, and slept in a large *pithos* ("pottery tub"). He destroyed his one drinking bowl when he realized he could drink water cupped in his own hands. Diogenes was famously outspoken, with a lack of shame that earned him the nickname "The Cynic" (originally meaning "dog"). Most Greeks were ashamed to beg, and found his behaviour shocking.

EPICURUS ▶

The most popular Greek philosopher was Epicurus of Samos (342–271 BC). He expressed ideas in aphorisms – brief sayings that were easy to memorize. He believed that the best way to avoid suffering was to lead a good life and to give up aims such as political ambition. His schools were unusual in being open to women and slaves as well as male citizens.

philosophy

Alexander with sword raised in battle

ALEXANDER THE GREAT

In the late 4th century BC, Greece was united under the leadership of Alexander, king of Macedon. Alexander, born in 356 BC, was the son of Philip II, who had already begun to unite the Greeks. By 334 BC, Alexander had built up an army of more than 37,000 men and crossed into Asia to invade Persia. After a series of victories, he controlled the world's most powerful empire. By his death, in 323 BC, he was known as Alexander the Great.

▲ BUCEPHALUS
This bronze statuette shows the young Alexander riding his horse, Bucephalus, which means ox-headed. The horse got its name because it had a wide, oxlike head. Alexander's first recorded achievement, at the age of 12, was to tame this horse, which nobody else had been able to ride. Bucephalus carried Alexander into many battles. The horse died in India in 326 BC. To honour Bucephalus, Alexander created a new town – named after the horse – at the place where it died.

Alexander

▲ MACEDONIANS
Although the Macedonians spoke Greek, they were looked down on by many Greeks (especially Athenians) as semibarbarians. Yet objects found in the royal tombs at Vergina show they had a sophisticated culture. This gold casket contained the cremated bones of Alexander's father Philip. The top is decorated with the emblem of the royal family – a starburst.

PHILIP ▶
Alexander's father, King Philip, paved the way for his military success. Philip created a powerful Macedonian army, which he used to conquer Thessaly and Thrace. He then forced all the leading Greek *poleis* (except Sparta) to join him in a military alliance. Philip planned to invade the Persian Empire but was murdered in 336 BC.

KING PHILIP

BATTLE OF ISSUS ▶
Alexander fought two major battles against the Persian king, Darius III, winning a decisive victory each time. This mosaic shows him at the moment of his victory over Darius in their first meeting, at the Battle of Issus (in Asia Minor) in 333 BC. Alexander, who has just speared a Persian cavalryman, gazes directly at Darius, who looks back at him in horror. Darius' charioteer desperately whips the horses, to escape from the battlefield. In the background, you can see long pikes, called *sarissas*, which were used by the Macedonian phalanx. This is thought to be a copy of a lost painting by the great Greek artist, Philoxenus.

Alexander

Pikes

Darius

Chari

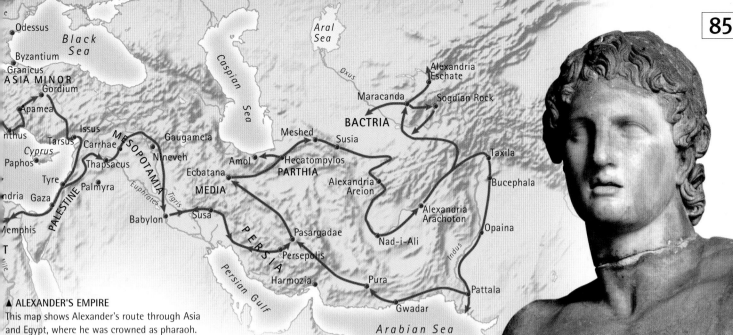

▲ ALEXANDER'S EMPIRE
This map shows Alexander's route through Asia and Egypt, where he was crowned as pharaoh. While conquering this empire, between 336 and 323 BC, he also founded 17 new towns which he called Alexandria after himself. He summoned Greeks and Macedonians to populate them.

▲ ALEXANDER'S REVENGE
After his final victory over Darius, the 25-year-old Alexander made himself ruler of the Persian Empire. This is the ruined palace of the Persian King Darius at Persepolis, which Alexander burned down following a drunken party. He claimed this was an act of revenge for the Greek temples burned by Xerxes in 480 BC.

▲ INTO INDIA
In 326 BC, Alexander invaded India and defeated King Porus, whose army included 100 elephants. However, after this conquest, Alexander's troops refused to go any further. Their spokesman, Coenus, told the king, "The one thing a successful man should know is when to stop!" This medallion shows an Indian war elephant.

Lion skin of Heracles

DEATH IN BABYLON ▶
When he left India, Alexander returned to his capital, Babylon, to plan new campaigns, against Arabia and North Africa. But in May 323 BC, he fell ill with a fever and died shortly afterwards. Alexander was so famous that even after his death, the kings who followed him continued to issue coins with his portrait. His face, with its jutting brow and straight nose, was known from Egypt to India.

LASTING FAME ▶
Alexander hoped to be remembered in history. On military campaigns, he took writers and poets with him to record his victories. He also had an official artist, Apelles, who painted his portrait, and a favourite sculptor, Lysippus, who carved statues of him. Although he ruled for only 13 years and died at just 32, Alexander's fame has lasted for 2,500 years.

THE HELLENISTIC AGE

After Alexander the Great's death, his empire broke up into separate kingdoms ruled by his generals, who called themselves kings. This was the start of a period known as the Hellenistic Age. It was a time when the Greek way of life spread throughout much of the ancient world, from Egypt to India. People learned to speak Greek, dress in Greek clothes, and live in Greek-style cities. They worshipped Greek gods, exercised in *gymnasia*, and watched tragedies and comedies at the theatre.

◀ **PLANNED CITIES**

Hellenistic rulers founded new cities, including Antioch in Syria and Pergamum and Ephesus in Asia Minor. These cities were planned using a grid layout with a network of streets crossing at right angles. Each city had an *agora*, temples, *gymnasia*, a theatre, and fortifications, like this tower at Priene in Asia Minor. Founded just before the Hellenistic Age, Priene is a typical Hellenistic city.

HELLENISTIC STATES

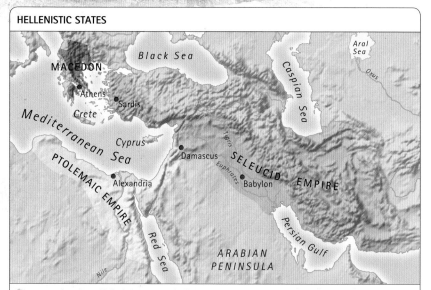

There were three large Hellenistic states – the Ptolemaic empire of Egypt, the Seleucid empire of Asia, and Macedonia. These were named after three of Alexander's generals – Ptolemy, Seleucus, and Antigonus. They were bitter rivals and fought a series of wars against each other. Antigonus hoped to rule the whole of Alexander's empire, but was killed at the Battle of Ipsus (in Asia Minor) in 301 BC. Antigonus II, his grandson, founded the Macedonian kingdom. Seleucus was murdered by a son of Ptolemy – the only one of the three not to die in battle. Alongside the three major kingdoms, there were several smaller ones.

GREEK KINGS

PTOLEMY
In 323 BC, Ptolemy made himself ruler of Egypt. He made himself ruler of Egypt, assuming the title of king in 305 BC. In temple art, he was shown as a traditional pharaoh, worshipping Egyptian gods. The Ptolemaic dynasty of Macedonian pharaohs, which he founded, ruled Egypt until 30 BC.

GREEK KINGS IN INDIA
This is a coin of Demetrius I, who invaded India in 200 BC and founded a Greek kingdom. His descendants ruled in northwest India for more than 150 years, preserving the Greek way of life – even though their kingdom was almost entirely cut off from the rest of the Greek world.

INTERNATIONAL LANGUAGE ►
During the Hellenistic age, Greek became an international language, spoken across the eastern Mediterranean and western Asia. As a result, in the 1st century AD, Jewish authors wrote the story of the life of Jesus Christ in Greek rather than the Hebrew of the Old Testament, or Aramaic – the language spoken by Jesus himself. The use of Greek meant that more people could read these writings.

Writing in the Codex Ebnerianus, a 12th-century AD Greek New Testament

e **Hellenistic Age**

◄ ART OF AGONY
During the Classical Age, Greek sculptors gave their statues perfect features and calm expressions. Hellenistic sculptors were more interested in depicting strong emotions. A famous example is the *Laocoon*, made by three sculptors from Rhodes – Hagesander, Athenodorus, and Polydorus. It shows the death agony of a Trojan prince and his sons, who, according to myth, were killed by two giant snakes. Their muscles strain and their faces grimace in pain.

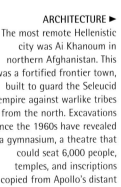

ART ►
The Greeks' lasting influence on Indian art can be seen in this statue of a Buddhist saint called a Bodhisattva. The realistic moulding of the body, the regular facial features, and the flowing drapery are all typical of Greek sculpture. This is combined with Indian characteristics, such as the hairstyle with its distinctive top knot and the heavy earrings – a mark of wealth and high status in India. Indian sculptors also carved Corinthian columns, copied from the Greeks.

ARCHITECTURE ►
The most remote Hellenistic city was Ai Khanoum in northern Afghanistan. This was a fortified frontier town, built to guard the Seleucid empire against warlike tribes from the north. Excavations since the 1960s have revealed a gymnasium, a theatre that could seat 6,000 people, temples, and inscriptions copied from Apollo's distant sanctuary at Delphi. These inscriptions were a set of sayings set up by a man called Clearchos, and they offered suggestions about how to live a good and moral life and then to "die without regret".

THE GREEK LEGACY

In the 2nd century BC, the Hellenistic kingdoms were conquered by the Romans who added Greece to their vast empire. The Romans were great admirers of Greek culture, and it was from Roman copies that western Europeans discovered Greek art and architecture. In the 18th century, there was a Greek revival when western Europeans first went to Greece to see original Greek art for themselves. Architecture is just one of many ways in which we are still influenced by the ancient Greeks.

▲ HADRIAN
The Roman Emperor Hadrian (AD 76–138) admired Greek culture so much that he was nicknamed "Graeculus" (meaning "the little Greek"). Hadrian spent four years in Greece, building more beautiful buildings in Athens. He even grew a beard to look more like the Greeks of the Classical Age.

Olympic torch

legacy

FRIEZE FROM THE PARTHENON

◄ OLYMPIC GAMES
In 1896, Pierre de Coubertin revived the Olympic Games as an international competition held every four years. The ancient games, he thought, could offer modern sport "a halo of grandeur and glory". Olympic events still include discus, javelin, and running races. The games always begin with the lighting of a flame from Olympia, which is carried by a runner to the site of the games.

▲ COLLECTORS
From the 18th century, the new interest in Greek art drew many rich visitors to Greece, which was then ruled by Turkey. The visitors took vases, statues, reliefs, and whole buildings, for private collections and public museums. In 1801, Lord Elgin stripped most of the sculptures from the Parthenon and these are still displayed in London's British Museum today. Many Greeks would like the sculptures returned.

THE GREEK REVIVAL

THE WHITE HOUSE
In the 1750s, two British architects, James Stuart and Nicholas Revett, published an illustrated book, *The Antiquities of Athens*, that started an international craze for Greek architecture. The White House in Washington, DC, in the USA, was designed in 1792 with an entrance modelled on an Ionic temple.

VALHALLA
The Valhalla in Regensburg, Germany, is a copy of the Parthenon, built in 1830-42 by the German king, Ludwig of Bavaria. Like the Parthenon, it marked a victory over a foreign invader – in this case, the French emperor, Napoleon. Ludwig filled it with statues of German heroes, including a large seated one of himself.

ATHENS 2004

▲ THE STARS

The names the ancient Greeks gave the constellations (groups of stars) in the night sky are still used today. This is Orion, named after a giant in a Boeotian myth. Orion was a mighty hunter, who boasted that he would kill all the wild beasts on earth. Artemis, protector of animals, sent a scorpion that stung and killed him and his dog Sirius. Orion still moves like a hunter across the night sky, followed by Sirius, and is chased by the constellation of Scorpio, the scorpion.

*Orion's belt
(three bright
stars in a row)*

Astrolabe

ARAB SCHOLARS ►

Greek culture was also passed to the western world by the Arabs, who conquered an empire stretching from Spain to Iraq in the 7th and 8th centuries AD. Arab scholars translated the works of Greek scientists and philosophers, including Ptolemy, Euclid, and Aristotle, into Arabic. In turn, these Arabic texts were translated into Latin by medieval Europeans. This illustration from a 14th-century Syrian book shows two Arab astronomers. One of them uses an astrolabe – an astronomical instrument invented by the Greeks to determine the sun's altitude.

Ballot box

▲ DEMOCRACY

Campaigners for political rights were inspired by Athenian democracy. Today, 120 of the world's 192 nations are democracies, although this word can be interpreted in different ways. Unlike Athens, with its direct democracy, today we have representative democracies. Decisions, such as going to war, are made by elected representatives rather than directly by the people. People make their wishes known by voting to elect the leader they want.

ACTING ►

When we watch actors today – on stage or in film and television – we see an art form invented by the ancient Greeks. Hollywood blockbusters and TV soap operas seem a long way from ancient Greek tragedies, but they still involve actors pretending to be characters in a story. Classic plays by the playwrights Aeschylus, Sophocles, Euripides, and Aristophanes are also still performed.

TIMELINE

This timeline shows the most important events in ancient Greek history, including major wars, and developments in art and science. All the dates listed are BC ("Before Christ"). Those dates with a "*c*", an abbreviation of "*circa*" (meaning "around"), before them indicate that the precise date of the event is unknown.

c.2900 The rise of Minoan civilization on Crete, where large complexes we call "palaces" are built at Knossos, Malia, and Phaestos.

c.1800 The Minoans invent Linear A, a writing system later adapted by the mainland Greeks. The Greek version of the script is called Linear B.

c.1600 The rise of Mycenaean civilization on mainland Greece, with palaces built at Mycenae, Tiryns, Pylos, Thebes, and Athens. Unlike Minoan palaces, these are heavily fortified.

c.1450 Mycenaean Greeks take over Knossos on Crete. We know this because the script used here changed from Linear A to Linear B at about this time.

c.1200–1150 The collapse of Mycenaean and Minoan civilizations, as the palaces are all destroyed by unknown enemies. Greece enters a "Dark Age".

c.1050 The Dorians, Greek-speaking people from the north, arrive in southern Greece. Iron is first used in Greece at about the same time and may have been introduced by the Dorians.

c.1000–900 Greeks from the mainland settle on the coasts and islands of Asia Minor. In the north, they are called Aeolians, and in the south, Ionians.

776 The first Olympic Games are held in honour of Zeus. The games, conducted every four years, give the Greeks a common dating system – numbered periods between the festivals are called *Olympiads*.

750–600 Greeks establish many settlements throughout the Mediterranean and Black Seas, including Syracuse in Sicily, Tarentum in southern Italy, and Massalia (Marseilles) in southern France.

c.750 Homer composes his epic poems, the *Iliad* and the *Odyssey*. At about the same time, the Greeks adapt the Phoenician alphabet to write Greek. We do not know whether Homer could write.

c.750 Foundation of Cumae, the earliest Greek settlement in Italy. The settlers come from Chalcis in Euboea, in western Greece. Cumae is 19 km (12 miles) west of Naples, another settlement founded by the Greeks.

735 Greeks from Chalcis, led by Thucles, found Naxos in Sicily – the earliest Greek settlement on the island.

734 Settlers from Corinth found Syracuse in western Sicily, which grows into the largest *polis* in the Greek world, and also one of the most powerful and wealthy.

706 The Spartans found their only overseas settlement, at Taras in southern Italy, known to the Romans as Tarentum (but today called Taranto).

c.700 "Black figure" vases, on which figures are painted black on a red or white background, are produced in Corinth.

c.700 Hesiod writes two poems. *Theogony* is about the birth of the gods. *Works and Days* is a guide to leading a good life through hard work.

c.650 The first Greek coins are made on the island of Aegina. The notion of manufacturing coins came from Lydia, in what is now Turkey.

c.620 Sappho of Lesbos is born. She writes poems that are widely admired and later collected into nine volumes.

c.620 Draco draws up the first law code of Athens. He calls for harsh punishments, with the death penalty for almost every offence. This is the origin of the word "draconian" (harsh or severe).

c.600 The Greeks start to build stone temples, developing the Doric style on the mainland, and the Ionic style in Ionia. The idea of building in stone rather than wood is thought to have come from Egypt.

594 The Athenian lawgiver, Solon, begins to draw up a new code of laws for Athens. He abolishes the harsher punishments of Draco.

558 The Persian Empire is founded by Cyrus the Great. The empire would later stretch from Egypt to Afghanistan and include the Greeks of Ionia.

c.525 The Athenians invent the "red figure" style of vase painting, in which figures are left in the red of the clay while the background is painted black.

508 The Athenians establish the first democracy following the expulsion of their last tyrant, Hippias. He escapes to Persia, where he encourages King Darius to invade Greece.

499 The Greeks of Ionia rebel against their Persian rulers. Despite help from Athens, the rebellion is crushed five years later.

499 The Athenian poet Aeschylus writes his first tragedy. He goes on to write between 70 and 90 more plays, winning 13 prizes in total for best playwright.

490 The Persian king Darius sends an invasion fleet to Greece to punish Athens for helping the Ionian rebellion. The Persian invaders are defeated by the Athenians and their allies from Plataea at the Battle of Marathon.

480 King Xerxes of Persia invades Greece with a new army and fleet. The Persians win a victory over the Spartans at Thermopylae, but their fleet is defeated at Salamis soon afterwards.

479 The Greek allies, led by the Spartans, win a final victory over the Persians at Plataea. This ends Xerxes' attempts to conquer Greece.

478 Athens becomes leader of the League of Delos – an alliance of *poleis* against Persia.

476 Cimon of Athens is chosen as general commanding the League's naval operations against Persia. Over the next 13 years, he drives the Persians from the coasts of Thrace and Ionia.

c.475 Polygnotus of Thasos produces his most famous paintings in Athens. Greatly admired by Greeks and Romans at the time, these paintings are now all lost.

468 The tragic playwright Sophocles competes against Aeschylus in the Athenian dramatic festival for the first time.

c.465 A major earthquake in Sparta results in the helots rebelling against their masters. The Spartans eventually crush the rebellion.

461 Cimon is ostracized from Athens. His enemy, Pericles, becomes the leading figure in Athenian politics.

460 The first war between Athens and Sparta begins, and neither side is able to win. The conflict lasts until 446 BC, ending Athens' attempt to establish an empire on the Greek mainland.

455 The Athenian playwright Euripides presents his first tragedy in the Athenian festival. He comes third.

454 Athenians move the treasury of the League from Delos to Athens for safekeeping. This gives Athens complete control over the finances of the League, which is transformed into an Athenian empire.

c.450 Herodotus of Helicarnassus writes the very first history book, based on an account of the Persian Wars. In Athens in the 440s, he gives readings from his work.

447–432 The Athenians rebuild the temples on the Acropolis, which had been destroyed by the Persians in 480 BC. The greatest temple is the Parthenon, a new marble temple for Athena.

431 The Peloponnesian War breaks out between Athens and Sparta. It is a much bigger conflict than the first war, and most of the Greek *poleis* are eventually forced to take one side or the other.

430 Plague breaks out in Athens, brought by a ship from the east. It spreads rapidly through the city, which is overcrowded with people from the countryside taking refuge from the Spartans.

427 The comic playwright Aristophanes produces his first work, *The Banqueters*, which is staged in Athens.

425 The Athenians win a victory over the Spartans on the island of Sphacteria, where 120 of the best Spartan warriors surrender.

416 The Athenians conquer Melos, killing all the men, and enslaving the women and children. The Melians had angered the Athenians by refusing to take sides in the war with Sparta.

415 Athens attempts to conquer Syracuse in Sicily. The invasion ends in disaster, with the loss of the entire army and fleet.

413 Sparta builds a permanent fort in Attica, at Deceleia. This serves as a place of refuge for thousands of slaves escaping from their Athenian owners.

405 The Spartans win a naval victory over Athens at Aegospotami. Without their fleet, the Athenians can no longer supply their city with food.

404 Following a long siege, Athens surrenders to Sparta. Sparta pulls down their defensive walls and overthrows the democracy, replacing it with an oligarchy.

403 The Athenians overthrow their oligarchic leaders, who have fallen out with each other, and reinstall the democracy.

c.400 Hippocrates, the "father of medicine", establishes a medical school on the Greek island of Cos. Many medical writings are later attributed to him.

c.400 Xenophon begins writing a history of the later stages of the war between Athens and Sparta. He goes on to write about many other subjects, including horse riding, politics, and his memories of Socrates.

399 The Athenian philosopher Socrates is sentenced to death for being a bad influence on the young. Socrates had made enemies by criticizing the democracy.

380 Socrates' greatest follower, Plato, founds a school in an Athenian gymnasium called the Academy. One of his pupils, studying here from 367–348 BC, is Aristotle.

371 The Thebans defeat the Spartans at the Battle of Leuctra, ending their supremacy in Greece. For a short period, Thebes is the most powerful *polis*.

359–336 Reign of King Philip of Macedon, whose kingdom becomes the strongest power in Greece. In 338 BC, he defeats the Thebans and Athenians at the Battle of Chaeronea.

336 Philip of Macedon is murdered by Pausanias, a Macedonian nobleman.

336 Alexander the Great, Philip's son, is crowned the new king of Macedon. He calls a meeting of the Greek *poleis* at Corinth, where he is confirmed as commander of the campaign against Persia.

335 Alexander fights rebels in Thrace, and the Greeks take advantage of his absence to rebel against him. He crushes the rebellion, sacking the leading *polis*, Thebes.

334 Alexander leads his vast army into Asia to begin his campaign against the Persian Empire. He wins his first victory over the Persians at the River Granicus.

333 Alexander defeats the Persian king Darius at the Battle of Issus. He then moves south, through Phoenicia.

332 Alexander captures the coastal cities of Tyre and Gaza, and then enters Egypt, where he is crowned as pharaoh.

331 After founding the city of Alexandria in Egypt, Alexander moves west again, winning his final victory over Darius at the Battle of Gaugamela. He enters Babylon, which he makes his capital.

327 Alexander begins a fresh campaign against India. The following year, his soldiers refuse to follow him any further, and he is forced to go back.

323 Alexander falls sick of a fever and dies in June.

322 Fighting breaks out between Alexander's rival generals. On one side are the commanders in Europe, Antipater and Craterus. On the other is Perdiccas, commander in Babylon.

304–292 The Colossus of Rhodes, a statue of the sun god Helios measuring 34 m (111 ft) in height, is built by Chares of Lindos. It is one of the Seven Wonders of the ancient world.

281 The wars between Alexander's successors end. There are now three Hellenistic kingdoms – the Antigonid kingdom of Macedonia, the Seleucid kingdom of Syria and Iraq, and the Ptolemaic kingdom of Egypt.

211 The mathematician, astronomer, and inventor, Archimedes, is killed by a Roman soldier during the capture of Syracuse.

c.200 Eratosthenes of Cyrene, a scientist working in Egypt, accurately calculates the size of the earth.

197–146 The Romans conquer Greece, in a series of wars against Macedon and the "Achaean League" of Greek *poleis* led by Corinth.

c.150–120 Polybius of Megalopolis, the last great Greek historian, writes a history of Rome's rise to power.

GLOSSARY

Acropolis Fortified area of a Greek city built on high ground. It means "high city".

Agora Greek term for the part of a *polis* where people gathered together. It was the main marketplace of a *polis*, and also included law courts and other public buildings.

Amphora Large, plain, two-handled pottery jar, used for storing oil, wine, and other goods.

Andron The "men's room" of a house, where the head of the house entertained his male friends.

Aulos Musical instrument in the form of a pair of pipes played with a reed.

Attica Territory around Athens.

Barbarian Greek name for a foreigner.

Black figure ware Pottery style in which figures are painted black on a red background.

Bronze Age Period when bronze was the main metal used for tools and weapons. In Greece, this lasted from about 3000–1100 BC.

Chiton Woman's tunic or dress.

Chorus Group of men who danced and spoke as one unit in a theatrical performance.

Citizen A free man with political rights in a state. Women and slaves were not considered citizens.

Classical Age Period between 500 and 300 BC, when the Greek *poleis* were at their height of power, and Greek civilization produced its greatest artists and writers.

Corinthian column Column with carved acanthus leaves at the top.

Democracy Rule by the people. Political system in which every male citizen could play an equal part in deciding how the *polis* was run. The citizens regularly met in assemblies, to speak and vote on important issues.

Dorians A Greek-speaking people originally from the northwest, who settled in Crete, Rhodes, and the Peloponnese from the 11th century BC.

Doric chiton A woman's sleeveless dress, created on the Greek mainland, where the Dorians lived.

Ephebe Youth aged between 18 and 20 – the ages of military training.

Gymnasium Centre where people practised athletics. *Gymnasia* could also be centres of learning, where lectures were given.

Hellenes Name used by the Greeks to refer to themselves. It comes from a legendary hero called Hellen, whom the Greeks thought of as their common ancestor.

Hellenistic Age Period following the death of Alexander the Great in 323 BC, when the Greek way of life was spread throughout the lands he had conquered.

Himation Large, loose, cloak worn by both men and women.

Hoplite Heavily armoured footsoldier who carried a spear and a shield called a *hoplon*.

Ionians A Greek people from the mainland who settled many of the islands and the southern coast of Asia Minor, later called Ionia.

Ionic column Column with a pair of scrolls carved at the top.

Krater Large decorated bowl used for mixing wine and water.

Libation Liquid offering – of wine, oil, milk, or blood – to a god, goddess, hero, and to the dead.

Linear A Writing system used on Crete by the Minoans. It is not understood by us today because its symbols have not yet been decoded.

Linear B Writing system, based on Linear A, used by the Mycenaeans to write Greek. Unlike Linear A, this system has been decoded.

Lyre Small, hand-held harp.

Minoan Early civilization of Crete, at its height between 2000 and 1450 BC.

Muses Nine goddesses who inspired the arts. It is from the muses that we get the words "music" and "museum" – originally from *mouseion*, a shrine to the muses.

Oligarchy Rule by the few. A system in which only the richest citizens of a *polis* could vote.

Omen Sign sent by a god, either to warn against disaster or to promise good luck.

Oracle Message thought to be given to people by a god in a particular holy place, such as Delphi. The word referred to both the place and the god's message.

Ostracism Athenian method of banishing (sending away) a citizen for ten years. This was a way of preventing any citizen becoming too powerful, rather than a form of punishment. People voted to ostracize citizens by writing names on *ostraka* (pieces of pottery).

Paidagogos Slave who looked after the young son or sons of his owner, taking them to school and watching over their behaviour there.

Palaestra Wrestling ground in a gymnasium.

Peloponnese Southern Greek mainland, named after a legendary king called Pelops. It is a peninsula, a piece of land almost surrounded by water, joined to the northern mainland by a narrow stretch of land.

Peltast Lightly armed warrior who used javelins (throwing spears) and carried a wickerwork shield called a *pelte*.

Phalanx Military formation in which soldiers marched together in close-packed ranks with shields and thrusting spears.

Pnyx Athenian hill where public assemblies met.

Polis Greek state comprising a single city and the surrounding farmland and villages.

Purification Ritual cleansing. The Greeks thought certain acts, such as shedding human blood, made people "unclean". They were unfit to worship their gods until they had purified themselves with rituals.

Pythia Title given to the priestess of Apollo at Delphi.

Red figure ware Style of pottery in which the figures are left in the red of the clay, while the background and details, such as lines for muscles, are painted black.

Relief Carving in which figures stand out from a flat background.

Rhyton Ceremonial drinking vessel, often with one end shaped like an animal or animal's head.

Sacrifice Gift to a god, especially an animal killed at an altar.

Stoa Long, roofed building with a wall on one side and a row of columns on the other. A *stoa* provided shade and shelter in a Greek *agora*.

Strategos Greek general. This is the origin of our word, "strategy", meaning military planning.

Terracotta Any object made of fired clay.

Tholos Circular building.

Trireme Warship with three banks of rowers.

Tyrant Ruler of a Greek *polis* who had seized power there, unlike a king, whose power was passed down through a family line.

WHO'S WHO

Aeschylus (525–456 BC)
The poet Aeschylus is the earliest writer of tragedies whose plays survive. Unlike previous writers, who used only one actor, Aeschylus used two. This made it possible for realistic dialogue and conflicts to take place.

Alcibiades (c.450–404 BC)
One of the leading generals during the war between Athens and Sparta, Alcibiades switched sides twice, fighting first on the Athenian side and then on the Spartan side, before finally rejoining the Athenians.

Alexander the Great (356–323 BC)
King of Macedon at the age of just 22, Alexander conquered the largest empire that the ancient world had seen. No other general of ancient times won as many victories.

Archimedes (c.287–212 BC)
Archimedes of Syracuse in Sicily was a great mathematician and inventor. During the Roman naval attack on Syracuse, he is said to have used large mirrors (possibly polished shields) to reflect sunlight onto the attacking ships, causing them to catch fire.

Aristophanes (c.445–c.385 BC)
In his lifetime, Aristophanes was known in Athens as the greatest writer of comedies. His plays were political and poked fun at living Athenians, and he was prosecuted for this more than once. Only 11 of his 40 plays survive today. These include *The Wasps* (422 BC), *The Birds* (414 BC), and *The Frogs* (405 BC).

Aristotle (384–322 BC)
Aristotle was a Greek philosopher, who studied under Plato and then opened his own school in Athens. He wrote about 400 books on a wide variety of subjects, including politics, biology, natural history, and poetry.

Cimon (c.510–c.450 BC)
Cimon was the most important Athenian general in the years between 478 and 463 BC, commanding most of the naval operations of the League of Delos against Persia. He drove the Persians out of Ionia and Thrace.

Euclid (c.300 BC)
Euclid was a mathematician who lived in Alexandria in Egypt in about 300 BC, but almost nothing is known of his life. Euclid's lasting fame comes from *The Elements*, his great textbook about mathematics.

Euripides (c.485–406 BC)
The youngest of the three great Athenian tragic playwrights (Aeschylus and Sophocles were the other two), Euripides wrote much darker plays than his rivals. Sophocles said that while he described people as they should be, Euripides showed people as they really were.

Herodotus (c.490–c.425 BC)
Herodotus of Helicarnassus wrote the first real history book, a vast work telling the story of the rise of the Persian Empire and the wars between Greece and Persia. It is also filled with accounts of the customs of different ancient peoples.

Hesiod (c.700 BC)
One of the earliest Greek poets, Hesiod wrote two long poems: the *Theogony*, about the birth of the gods, and *Works and Days*, a poem giving advice regarding practical matters, such as running a farm.

Hippocrates (c.460–c.370 BC)
The most famous doctor of the ancient world, Hippocrates of Cos introduced new scientific methods for treating the sick. He also created a code of behaviour for medical students, who had to swear to do their best for their patients. This is still used today.

Homer (c.750 BC)
Homer was the author of the *Iliad* and the *Odyssey*, two long poems based on the legend of the Trojan War. Regarded as the greatest poems of the ancient world, they have never lost their popularity, from Homer's time to our own.

Lysander (d. c.395 BC)
Lysander was the greatest Spartan general during the last stages of the Peloponnesian War. In 405 BC, he caught the Athenians by surprise at Aegospotami and captured their whole fleet while it was still on the beaches. This led to the final downfall of Athens.

Miltiades (c.550–448 BC)
The Athenian general Miltiades was the commander at the Battle of Marathon (490 BC). Miltiades led the Athenian army and the Plataean allies to a great victory over the Persian invaders.

Pausanias (d. 470 BC)
The Spartan general Pausanias commanded the allied Greek army that won a final victory over the Persian invaders at the battle of Plataea in 479 BC. Later accused of treason, Pausanias took refuge in a Spartan temple, where he was starved to death.

Pericles (c.495–429 BC)
The most famous Athenian politician of his time, Pericles dominated Athens from around 461 BC until his death. He helped create the Athenian empire, and persuaded his fellow citizens to build magnificent new temples, such as the Parthenon.

Phidias (c.490–c.432 BC)
The Athenian sculptor Phidias was the most famous Greek artist. His masterpiece was the statue of Zeus at Olympia, one of the Seven Wonders of the ancient world. Phidias also created the sculpture for the Parthenon, including its gold and ivory statue of Athena.

Plato (c.427–347 BC)
The philosopher Plato founded the Academy, a famous school of philosophy located in Athens. He wrote more than 20 books, in which his teacher, Socrates, plays the central role.

Pythagoras (6th century BC)
Pythagoras was a mathematician and religious teacher who lived on Samos. Through mathematical study, he hoped to unlock the secrets of the universe.

Sappho (b. c.620)
Sappho was a poet who lived on Lesbos and wrote many short poems during the 6th century BC. She is one of the few female writers from ancient times whose works have survived and are still read today.

Socrates (469–399 BC)
Socrates was an Athenian philosopher. Although he wrote no books, he had a huge influence through his teaching and the moral way in which he lived his life. His central belief was that those who understood the difference between right and wrong would not act badly.

Solon (c.640–560 BC)
Solon was an Athenian poet. He drew up a humane code of laws and reforms for the Athenians, hoping to find a middle way between the demands of the rich and poor. His laws laid the foundation for later concepts of democracy.

Sophocles (c.496–405 BC)
One of the great Athenian tragic playwrights, Sophocles used three actors in his plays – only one or two had been used before – to create more complex dramas.

Thales (c.585 BC)
Thales of Miletus was considered the first Greek philosopher. He was also a scientist. He predicted an eclipse of the sun, which took place in 585 BC.

Themistocles (c.524–c.459 BC)
Themistocles was an Athenian statesman and general, who persuaded his fellow Athenians to build up their war fleet, and then led them to victory over the Persians at the Battle of Salamis in 480 BC.

Thucydides (c.455–c.399 BC)
Thucydides was an Athenian general and author of a history of the Peloponnesian War. Although influenced by Herodotus, he did not share the older historian's belief that the gods played a role in human affairs.

INDEX

A page number in **bold** refers to the main entry for that subject.

ACKNOWLEDGEMENTS

Dorling Kindersley Ltd would like to thank Marion Dent for proof-reading; Michael Dent for the index; Constance Novis for Americanizing; and Leah Germann, Elizabeth Healey, and Ralph Pitchford for design support. Thanks also to Jane Chapman.

Dorling Kindersley Ltd is not responsible and does not accept liability for the availability or content of any website other than its own, or for any exposure to offensive, harmful or inaccurate material that may appear on the internet. Dorling Kindersley Ltd will have no liability for any damage or loss caused by viruses that may be downloaded as a result of looking at and browsing the websites that it recommends. Dorling Kindersley downloadable images are the sole copyright of Dorling Kindersley Ltd and may not be reproduced, stored, or transmitted in any form or by any means for any commercial or profit-related purpose without prior written permission of the copyright owner.

Picture Credits

The publisher would like to thank the following for their kind permission to reproduce their photographs:

Abbreviations key

t-top, b-bottom, r-right, l-left, c-centre, ftl-far top left, tl-top left, tc-top centre, tr-top right, ftr-far top right; fcla-far centre left above, cla-centre left above, ca-centre above, cra-centre right above, fcra-far centre right above; fcl-far centre left; cl-centre left, cr-centre right, fcr-far centre right; fclb-far centre left below, clb-centre left below, cb-centre below, crb-centre right below, fcrb-far centre right below, fbl-far bottom left, bl-bottom left, bc-bottom centre, br-bottom right, fbr-far bottom right.

8 akg-images/John Hios tr; Ancient Art and Architecture Collection c. 8-9 The Art Archive/Dagli Orti b. 9 Corbis Sygma/Attar Maher tl; Corbis/Araldo de Luca; DK Images/Archaeological Receipts Fund (TAP)/Max Alexander tr; Ancient Art and Architecture Collection cra; DK Images/British Museum cr; The Art Archive/Musée du Louvre, Paris/Dagli Orti b. 10 The Art Archive/Bibliothèque des Arts Décoratifs, Paris/Dagli Orti tl; Ancient Art and Architecture Collection r; DK Images/Archaeological Receipts Fund (TAP)/Max Alexander b. 11 Bildarchiv Preußischer Kulturbesitz; Ancient Art and Architecture Collection tl; Ancient Art and Architecture Collection cr; Ancient Art and Architecture Collection r; Ancient Art and Architecture Collection br; 12 Ancient Art and Architecture Collection t; The Art Archive/Archaeological Museum, Chora/Dagli Orti cl; DK Images/Archaeological Receipts Fund (TAP) bl. 12-13 DK Images/Archaeological Receipts Fund (TAP)/Joe Cornish b. 13: The Art Archive/Dagli Orti tl; The Art Archive/National Archaeological Museum, Athens/Dagli Orti tr; Ancient Art and Architecture Collection cr; The Art Archive/National Archaeological Museum, Athens/Dagli Orti br; Bildarchiv Preußischer Kulturbesitz fbr. 14 Photo Scala, Florence/Museo Nazionale, Naples tl; akg-images/Erich Lessing tr; The Art Archive c; Bridgeman Art Library/Staatliche Museen, Berlin bl. 14-15 Ronald Grant Archive/Warner Bros b. 15 akg-images/Nimatallah tl; Bildarchiv Preußischer Kulturbesitz tr; akg-images/Erich Lessing cr; Bridgeman Art Library/Le Louvre, Paris br. 16 By kind permission of the Trustees of the National Gallery, London/Corbis t; Bridgeman Art Library/British Museum, London b. 17 Gianni Dagli Orti/Corbis; José F.Poblete/Corbis cl; akg-images/Erich Lessing ftr; akg-images/Erich Lessing fcra, Photo RMN/Hervé Lewandowski fcr; Photo RMN/Hervé Lewandowski fcrb; The Art Archive/Bibliothèque des Arts Décoratifs, Paris/Dagli Orti fbr. 18 Corbis/Sandro Vannini tl; Photo RMN/ Hervé Lewandowski tr; akg-images b. 18-19 The Art Archive/Dagli Orti c. 19 The Art Archive/ Archaeological Museum, Corinth/Dagli Orti bl; The Art Archive/The National Archaeological Museum, Athens/Dagli Orti bc, akg-images br. 20 The Art Archive/Dagli Orti t; Photo RMN/ Hervé

Lewandowski c; akg-images/Peter Connolly b. 21 Bildarchiv Preußischer Kulturbesitz tl; The Art Archive/Archaeological Museum, Naples/Dagli Orti(A) tr; The Art Archive/National Glyptothek, Munich/Dagli Orti(A) bl; The Art Archive/Jan Vinchon Numimatist, Paris/Dagli Orti cra; Ancient Art and Architecture Collection cr; The Art Archive/ Jan Vinchon Numimatist, Paris/Dagli Orti br; 22 Bridgeman Art Library/Le Louvre, Paris b; 22-23 Pat Behnke/Alamy c. 23 British Museum, London cl; Bridgeman Art Library/British Museum, London c; Bildarchiv Preußischer Kulturbesitz b. 24 Corbis/Yann Arthus-Bertrand t; Ancient Art and Architecture Collection cl; Bridgeman Art Library/ British Museum, London br. 25 akg-images/ Nimatallah tl; Ancient Art and Architecture Collection c; Corbis/Paul A.Souders b; Corbis/Archivo Iconografico S.A./Corbis cla. 26 Topfoto/HIP/British Museum tr, akg-images/Peter Connolly b. 27 Corbis/ Stephanie Colasanti t; akg-images/Nimatallah cl; akg-images/John Hios c; akg-images/John Hios b; akg-images clb; Bridgeman Art Library/Galleria degli Uffizi, Florence b. 28 Ancient Art and Architecture Collection c; Ancient Art and Architecture Collection c; akg-images/John Hios b. 29 Photo Scala, Florence/Gregorian Museum of Etruscan Art, Vatican tl; Photo RMN/ Hervé Lewandowski tc; Photo RMN/ Hervé Lewandowski tr; Bridgeman Art Library/Private Collection cl; Ancient Art and Architecture Collection cr; The Art Archive/Musée du Louvre, Paris/Dagli Orti b. 30 akg-images/Erich Lessing l; Ancient Art and Architecture Collection r; akg-images/Erich Lessing bl; akg-images/Nimatallah b. 31 Hulton Archive/ Getty Images tl; Corbis/ Jacqui Hurst tr; National Trust Photo Library/Stourhead/John Hammond bl; Photo RMN/ Hervé Lewandowski br. 32 Ancient Art and Architecture Collection l. 32-33 Bildarchiv Preußischer Kulturbesitz b. 33 The Art Archive/ Musée du Louvre, Paris/Dagli Orti tl; Charlie Best tc; akg-images/Nimatallah tr; Ancient Art and Architecture Collection bl; Ancient Art and Architecture Collection br; 34: The Art Archive/ Archaeological Museum, Naples/Dagli Orti t; Charlie Best c. 34-35 Lebrecht Music and Arts b. 35 The Art Archive/Archaeological Museum, Naples/Dagli Orti tl; Bridgeman Art Library/Ashmolean Museum, Oxford tc; akg-images/Erich Lessing tr; Corbis/ Mimmo Jodice cl; Corbis/Christie's Images cr. 36 akg-images/Erich Lessing c; akg-images/Peter Connolly bl; akg-images/Peter Connolly br. 36-37 Corbis/Gianni Dagli Orti t; Photo Scala, Florence/National Museum, Reggio Calabria, Italy cl; Ancient Art and Architecture Collection c; Ancient Art and Architecture Collection cr; akg-images/Erich Lessing bl; Ancient Art and Architecture Collection br. 38 The Art Archive/Kerameikos Museum, Athens/ Dagli Orti l; Photo Scala, Florence/Museo Archeologico, Ferrara, Italy r. 39 Charlie Best tl; The Art Archive/Archaeological Museum, Florence/Dagli Orti tc; Charlie Best tr; Mary Evans Picture Library bl; The Art Archive/Museo di Villa Giulia, Rome/Dagli Orti br. 40 The Art Archive/Musée du Louvre, Paris/ Dagli Orti t; Bildarchiv Preußischer Kulturbesitz bl; The Art Archive/Archaeological Museum, Naples/ Dagli Orti br. 41 Ancient Art and Architecture Collection tl; The Art Archive/Archaeological Museum, Spina Ferrara/Dagli Orti(A) tr; Ancient Art and Architecture Collection cl; Ancient Art and Architecture Collection bl; The Art Archive/ Goulandris Foundation, Athens/Dagli Orti br. 42 Photo Scala, Florence/Museo Pio-Clementino, Vatican l; Photo Scala, Florence/Museum of the Agora, Athens c; The Art Archive/Dagli Orti br. 43 Bildarchiv Preußischer Kulturbesitz tl; akg-images c; Corbis/Roger Wood tr. 44 The Art Archive/Archaeological Museum, Istanbul/Dagli Orti l; The Art Archive/Museo Statale Metaponto/Dagli Orti tr; Bildarchiv Preußischer Kulturbesitz c; Ancient Art and Architecture Collection b. 45 DK Images/ The British Museum cla; DK Images/The British Museum cl; DK Images/The British Museum clb; Photo RMN/ Hervé Lewandowski b; Museum of Classical Archaeology, Cambridge br. 46 Bridgeman Art Library/Le Louvre, Paris t; akg-images/Erich Lessing bl; Ancient Art and Architecture Collection br. 47 akg-images/Erich Lessing tl; akg-images/Peter Connolly bl; David Gill cra; akg-images/Erich Lessing cr; Ancient Art and Architecture Collection crb; akg-

images/Erich Lessing br. 48 Getty Images/Charlie Waite bl; akg-images/Erich Lessing br. 49 Bridgeman Art Library/Freud Museum, London ftl; Bridgeman Art Library/Ashmolean Museum, Oxford tl; Photo RMN/ Hervé Lewandowski tr; Bridgeman Art Library/Fitzwilliam Museum, University of Cambridge ftr; akg-images/Erich Lessing cl; Photo RMN/Hervé Lewandowski cr; The Art Archive/Archaeological Museum, Ferrara/Dagli Orti(A) b. 50 The Art Archive/Dagli Orti t; British Museum, London bl; The Art Archive/Jan Vinchon Numismatist, Paris/Dagli Orti(A) br. 51 Corbis/ Jonathan Blair tl; The Art Archive/Archaeological Museum, Florence/Dagli Orti tc; Corbis/James Davis/ Eye Ubiquitous tr. 52 The Art Archive/Acropolis Museum, Athens/Dagli Orti tl; Corbis/Vanni Archive bl; Bridgeman Art Library/Le Louvre, Paris br. 52-53 Corbis/Robert Gill, Papilio. 53 Corbis/Mimmo Jodice tl; Photo Scala/Bargello, Florence clb; akg-images/Andrea Baguzzi bl; Corbis/Gianni Dagli Orti r 54 Bildarchiv Preußischer Kulturbesitz tl; akg-images/Nimatallah r; The Art Archive/Bibliothèque des Arts Décoratifs, Paris/Dagli Orti. 55 Photo Scala, Florence/National Archaeological Museum, Athens tl; akg-images/Erich Lessing cla; Bridgeman Art Library/ Le Louvre cl; akg-images/Erich Lessing clb; akg-images/Erich Lessing bl; Ancient Art and Architecture Collection tr; Bernhard Edmaier/Science Photo Library bl. 56 Corbis/Wolfgang Kaehler tr; Ancient Art and Architecture Collection cr; Ancient Art and Architecture Collection cr; Bildarchiv Preußischer Kulturbesitz bl. 57 Bildarchiv Preußischer Kulturbesitz tl; Getty Images/Chris Hackett tr; Getty Images/Victoria Pearson cra; Ancient Art and Architecture Collection crb; Ancient Art and Architecture Collection br; The Art Archive/Musée du Louvre, Paris/Dagli Orti bl. 58 akg-images/Erich Lessing l; Ancient Art and Architecture Collection tr; The Art Archive/Archaeological Museum, Naples/ Dagli Orti b. 59 akg-images/Erich Lessing tl; Corbis/ Massimo Listri tr; Photo Scala, Florence, Museo Archeologico, Ferrara, Italy c; The Art Archive/ National Archaeological Museum/Dagli Orti fbl; akg-images/Nimatallah bl; Bildarchiv Preußischer Kulturbesitz bc; Ancient Art and Architecture Collection br. 60 akg-images/Nimatallah tl; akg-images/Erich Lessing tr; akg-images/Peter Connolly cr. 60-61 Corbis/Adam Woolfitt b. 61 The Bridgeman Art Library/Private Collection tl; The Art Archive/Acropolis Museum, Athens/Dagli Orti tr; Topfoto/HIP/British Museum cr; Ancient Art and Architecture Collection cl; Bridgeman Art Library br. 62 The Art Archive/Dagli Orti l; Ancient Art and Architecture Collection tr; Bridgeman Art Library/Le Louvre, Paris, cr. 63 akg-images/Gérard Degeorge tl; akg-images/Peter Connolly cl; akg-images/ Nimatallah br. 64 Corbis/Werner Forman tl; Ancient Art and Architecture Collection cl. 65 Photo RMN/ Hervé Lewandowski tl; Bridgeman Art Library/ National Museum of Scotland tr; The Art Archive/ Agora Museum, Athens/Dagli Orti c; akg-images/ Peter Connolly b. 66 Ancient Art and Architecture Collection cl; Corbis/Mimmo Jodice cr. 67 Ancient Art and Architecture Collection tc; Corbis/Archivo Iconografico, S.A cr; Photo Scala, Florence/Museo Nazionale, Naples, br; Ancient Art and Architecture Collection bl; Ancient Art and Architecture Collection tl; Ancient Art and Architecture Collection bl. 68-69 Ancient Art and Architecture Collection t; Corbis/James Davis/Eye Ubiquitous b. 69 akg-images/Peter Connolly cr. 70 akg-images/Erich Lessing cl. 70-71 The Art Archive/Archaeological Museum, Piraeus/Dagli Orti. 71 Bridgeman Art Library/Ashmolean Museum/University of Oxford tr; Bridgeman Art Library/Galleria degli Uffizi, Florence clb; Bridgeman Art Library/Tamashagah-e Pool, Tehran cb; Mary Evans Picture Library br. 72 Corbis/ Archivo Iconografico S.A. tl; Bridgeman Art Library cr; Bridgeman Art Library/Ashmolean Museum, University of Oxford bl; The Art Archive/Musée du Louvre, Paris/Dagli Orti br. 73 Corbis/Gianni Giansanti/Sygma l; Mary Evans Picture Library tr; akg-images/Peter Connolly br. 74 akg-images; DK Images/Archaeological Receipts Fund (TAP)/Joe Cornish tr; Corbis/Yann Arthus-Bertrand bl. 74-75 Corbis/Araldo de Luca tr. 75 akg-images/ Nimatallah tl; DK Images/British Museum cl; Bridgeman Art Library/British Museum, London bl;

images/Erich Lessing br. 48 Getty Images/Charlie Waite bl; akg-images/Erich Lessing br.

The Art Archive/Musée du Louvre, Paris/Dagli Ortis ftr; Ancient Art and Architecture Collection fcra; Topfoto/HIP/Ann Ronan Picture Library fcr; Bridgeman Art Library/Museo Nazionale Romano, Rome fcrb; The Art Archive/Bibliothèque des Arts Décoratifs, Paris/Dagli Orti fbr. 76 DK Images/The British Museum tl; The Art Archive/Archaeological Museum, Piraeus/Dagli Orti tr; Corbis/Sandro Vannini b. 77 Art Resource, New York tl; DK Images/The Nicholas P.Goulandris Foundation/Museum of Cycladic Art, Athens tc; Ancient Art and Architecture Collection tr; The Art Archive/Siritide Museum, Policoro/Dagli Orti cl; The Art Archive/Museo Capitolino, Rome/Dagli Orti cra; Ancient Art and Architecture Collection cr; The Bridgeman Art Library/Museo Archeologico Nazionale, Naples crb; Corbis/Robbie Jack bl. 78 The Art Archive/Museo Capitolino, Rome/Dagli Orti(A) tl; Corbis/Archivo Iconografico, S.A bl; Photo Scala, Florence/Ducal Palace, Urbino, Italy bl. 79 The Art Archive/ Museo Nazionale Romano, Rome/Dagli Orti(A) tr; Bridgeman Art Library/Pushkin Museum, Moscow fbl; Topfoto/HIP/Ann Ronan Picture Library bl; Ancient Art and Architecture Collection br; akg-images/Erich Lessing fbr. 80 The Art Archive/Museo Nazionale Palazzo Altemps, Rome/Dagli Orti tl; Ancient Art and Architecture Collection tr; The Art Archive/Archaeological Museum, Piraeus/Dagli Orti bl. 81 akg-images/Erich Lessing tl; akg-images/Erich Lessing tc; Ancient Art and Architecture Collection bl; The Wellcome Trust Medical Photographic Library bc; akg-images/Rabatti-Domingie br. 82 Corbis/ Araldo de Luca tl; Time Life Pictures/Getty Images tr Getty Images fbl; akg-images bl; Corbis/Mimmo Jodice br; akg-images/Nimatallah fbr. 83 Corbis/ Alinari Archives tl; Bridgeman Art Library/Walters Art Museum, Baltimore cl; Ancient Art and Architecture Collection b. 84 Ancient Art and Architecture Collection tl; The Art Archive/Archaeological Museum, Salonica/Dagli Orti cl; The Art Archive/ Chiaramonti Museum, Vatican/Dagli Orti(A) cr; Ancient Art and Architecture Collection b. 85 Corbis/Jose Fuste Rasa cl; The Art Archive c; akg-images cr; akg-images b. 86-87 Corbis/Araldo de Luca b. 87 Topfoto tl; Topfoto/HIP/The British Museum tc; The Art Archive/Bodleian Library, Oxford tr; Ancient Art and Architecture Collection cr. 88 Corbis/Dimitris Doudoumis tl; Corbis/Araldo de Luca tr; Michael Booth/Alamy c; Corbis/Lester Lefkowitz bc; Corbis/Hilbich br. 89 NASA t; Corbis/David Turnley cl; Ancient Art and Architecture Collection cr; Corbis/Layne Kennedy br.

Jacket images

Front Corbis: Charles O'Rear cr; Jon Hicks fcl; DK Images: Archaeological Receipts Fund cl; The Art Archive: Archaeological Museum Naples/Dagli Orti fcr. **Spine** DK Images: Archaeological Receipts Fund. **Back** Corbis: Larry Lee Photography fcr; Getty Images: Stone cl; The Bridgeman Art Library cr, fcl.

All other images © Dorling Kindersley. For further information see: www.dkimages.com